The Shingo Production Management System

The Shingo Production Management System

Improving Process Functions

SHIGEO SHINGO

Translated by Andrew P. Dillon

Publisher's Message by
Norman Bodek

Productivity Press
Portland, Oregon

Originally published as *Seisan kanri no kakumei to kōtei kinō no kaizen* by Japan Management Association, Tokyo © 1990.

English translation by Andrew P. Dillon copyright © 1992 by Productivity, Inc.

Productivity, Inc.
P.O. Box 13390
Portland, OR 97213-0390
United States of America
Telephone: 503-235-0600
Telefax: 503-235-0909
E-mail: info@productivityinc.com

Cover design by Gail Graves
Printed and bound by BookCrafters
Printed in the United States of America

Library of Congress Cataloging-in-Publication Data

Shingō, Shigeo, 1909–1990
   [Seisan kanri no kakumei to kōtei kinō no kaizen. English]
   The Shingo production management system : improving process functions / Shigeo Shingo; translated by Andrew P. Dillon.
       p.   cm.
   Translation of: Seisan kanri no kakumei to kōtei kinō no kaizen.
   Includes index.
   ISBN 0-915299-52-6
   1. Production management. I. Title
   TS155.S461513   1992
   658.5—dc20   91-34857
                                                              CIP

05 04 03 02 01 00   12 11 10 9 8 7

Contents

Illustrations

Publisher's Message

When Shigeo Shingo passed away in 1990 at the age of 81, he left a legacy of accomplishments behind him. He was the author of more than 25 books on manufacturing improvement and an international consultant to some of the world's largest companies. Honda, Toyota, Bridgestone Tire, Hewlett-Packard, Peugeot, Kentucky Fried Chicken, and AT&T are just a few of the firms at which he inspired change. *The Shingo Production Management System: Improving Process Functions* was the last book he wrote, and I am honored to publish it in English.

Dr. Shingo developed and perfected a methodology to improve manufacturing processes. Through his careful study of existing manufacturing conditions he noted fundamental wastes, fundamental misconceptions of how goods and services were being delivered by by industry. While almost every other manager in the world accepted large batch sizes, economic order quantities, long setup times, defective products, existing inspection systems, and underutilized workers, Shingo conceived of a new way to improve almost to perfection the manufacturing process and its operations. From the body of his life's works — including just-in-time (JIT), the SMED system, and the *poka-yoke* system — a revolution has taken place on the factory floor.

On my last trip to Japan I again visited the best example of Dr. Shingo's work — the Matsushita washing machine plant outside of Shizuoka. Over 5,500 washing machines a day are produced with a total staff of only 408 people, which includes administration, management, and software engineers. It takes three and a half hours from raw steel to finished painted machine — it is the most productive washing machine plant in the world. Amazingly, this plant has none of the kanban carts normally seen in other JIT factories.

It is a CIM/JIT plant that produces in-house every major part in one-piece flow and machining. Computer workstations are located next to the assembly lines to handle almost daily changes to the process. Operators are informed instantly through individual CRTs in front of them on every detail about the machine they are working on. There is no maintenance department — operators receive instruction in how to fix their own machines. There are 550 *poka-yoke* mistake-proofing devices installed along the manufacturing process to prevent defects. The Matsushita plant represents Dr. Shingo's dream to eliminate all non-value-adding wastes in the manufacturing process.

I last saw Dr. Shingo in September 1990 in Japan prior to his death. At lunch in a Fujisawa restaurant near his home I watched him rise with great difficulty and move slowly from his wheelchair to the table. His body had deteriorated quickly that past year but his mind was as sharp as ever. Once he sat down he was again teaching me his concepts. He was persistent in his desire to teach the world to see manufacturing processes rather than separate operations. He was relentless and also hopeful, believing that once senior management really understood these concepts, they could drastically change their manufacturing processes.

It was a great privilege for me to know Dr. Shingo personally. In 1981 on a study mission to Japan, I discovered his book, *The Study of the Toyota Production System from an Industrial Engineering Viewpoint*. I called him and received permission to distribute his book in the United States. He subsequently asked me to translate and publish all of his current books and training materials into English.

I saw Dr. Shingo dramatically demonstrate many times in factories how to reduce setup times from hours to minutes. It was not that he particularly liked doing this. It was simply his understanding that people would not believe his methodology unless they saw it with their own eyes. At one plant I saw a setup that averaged 4 hours. When Dr. Shingo asked the group to do it in less than 10 minutes, they looked very skeptical. But then he showed them how to standardize die heights and reduce cam adjustment, improve clamping, eliminate further adjustments, and ease movement and searching. After his brief lecture, 2 hours later the workers performed the setup in 12 minutes. Dr. Shingo was pleased but encouraged them next time to do it in less than 10 minutes.

A month ago I saw a 6-spindle boring machine and asked the operator how long it took to make a changeover. His reply was 8 to 12 hours. Shortly thereafter, I discovered that the same machine can be changed in under an hour without a major overhaul and that with some structural changes the changeover can be further reduced to minutes. The question then is why isn't it being done? Why do we still allow archaic practices to rule the factory floor? I can understand Dr. Shingo's frustration as he traveled around the world trying to convince managers and engineers that JIT was both practical and doable.

He was a universalist and wanted to improve the world's manufacturing, not just Japan's. He felt that if managers and operators understood the difference between process and operations, they could make giant improvements. This book is dedicated to that principle.

Dr. Shingo always talked and wrote about improving production management. However, while his previous books are written from an "operations" perspective, *The Shingo Production Management System* focuses on "processes." In this, his final book, he wanted to provide a basis of understanding for serious production managers and scholars about what a comprehensive map of production functions would look like — not about the specific improvement operations such as SMED, ZQC, and *poka-yoke* discussed in his previous books. He taught that before production management could be improved, two things had to be understood clearly: (1) what a production management system is and (2) how to carry out improvements.

Dr. Shingo believed that the reason improvement concepts such as source inspection systems and non-stock production did not originate in the West was because the improvement-oriented ideas of Frank Gilbreth and others did not really sink in. To this end, he includes a chapter on his "Scientific Thinking Mechanism" (STM) for improvement.

This book comprises 7 parts and 17 chapters. Part I presents problems and approaches to improvement. Following a review of Hawthorne, MacGregor, and others, Dr. Shingo concludes that a number of deficiencies in conventional production management philosophy must be corrected immediately. He offers a glimpse of how some U.S. companies are improving right now — companies such as Granville-Phillips, United Electric Controls, and Globe Metal Alloy.

Part II discusses the fundamental thinking necessary for improving production management. He emphasizes that Gilbreth's concepts are not outdated but still mark the point of departure for improvement. The author's "Scientific Thinking Mechanism" (STM) system for improvement is an extension of Gilbreth's ideas. He reiterates that understanding the basic techniques of how improvement should be carried out is at the heart of production management improvement.

He discusses specific tools for putting together an improvement plan: observation, idea formulation, judgment, suggestion, and implementation. He then turns to the basic flaws in conventional production management improvement, insisting that a critical review of current production systems is important in understanding these flaws. He states that all improvements are not equal; that how we look at improvement objectives determines the kind of improvements we end up with. Too often, he adds, we fail to question the function of existing machinery — and he presents examples.

Part III focuses on the object of improvement — the structure and functions of production. Exploiting demand is the first step in production management. Clarifying and exploiting potential market needs and altering needs for existing models are two issues to study from the perspective of value engineering and value analysis. Dr. Shingo examines management's five functional aspects (technical skills, finance, production, marketing, and personnel) and management's seven action stages (wanting, deciding, planning, implementing, controlling, monitoring, and satisfaction). He talks about how techniques such as CAD/CAM can be effective at the design-generating stage. He emphasizes that, to avoid nonessential information, information management is essential.

In Part IV, process functions are expressed by four different phenomena: processing, inspection, transportation, and delays. He switches from talking about process improvement for single parts to talking about improving process control systems for assembly in large-lot production, flow systems, process-type synchronization, mixed production systems, block production, the supermarket system, and multimachine and multiprocess handling systems.

Until now, efforts to improve production functions have concentrated solely on upgrading operations functions. Part V focuses on operational improvement and why Dr. Shingo thinks process functions should take precedence over operational functions. He talks about how the division of labor in eighteenth-century England affected the development of work. He then looks at types of operations including setup improvement, operational functions, mechanization of manual functions, the automation of manual functions and operational improvements through robotization and pre-automation, total productive maintenance (TPM) and skills management, improving and dealing with human nature, and the pack system.

Parts VI and VII present his steps to improving productivity worldwide and his final thoughts on improving productivity in the future. An appendix gives a chronological development of management thought from 1750 to 1990.

I cannot say enough about my regard for this genius. He was both friend and teacher, and I was privileged to accompany him on many consultations to companies around the world. He was held in high esteem by everyone who ever met him — and many moments of his inspiration remain vivid for me. It is now up to us to continue to spread his teachings. Western manufacturers are proving each day that his concepts work here. Each is a value-adding tool that increases productivity.

I hope that you will find the ideas presented in this book to be a valuable gift from an industrial genius. His name already ranks with the innovative likes of Eli Whitney, Henry Ford, and Thomas Edison. Dr. Shingo would only ask that you study and then quickly apply these ideas in your workplace.

Many people made the production of this English edition possible. My sincere gratitude goes to Hiroshi Shimizu, director, and Kazuya Uchiyama, assistant director, of the Publication and Information Development Division of the Japan Management Association. In the United States, Steven Ott, vice president of Productivity Press, arranged for its publication. The book was translated by Andrew Dillon, and Cheryl Rosen managed the developmental edit. Bill Berling copyedited the book; Phyllis Lindsay proofread the galleys; and Jennifer Cross provided the index. Joyce C. Weston designed the cover. Guided by Gayle Joyce, the production staff for the book included Jane Worcester and Michele Saar.

Norman Bodek
Publisher

Preface

At one point during a trip to the United States in April 1988, I remember being taken aback at a question put to me by Norman Bodek, president of Productivity, Inc. "What you are telling me now about making production more rational," Mr. Bodek said, "is somewhat different from what you told me three days ago. Why?" I replied that my explanation three days earlier had been from the perspective of production *operations* and that now I was discussing the question from the standpoint of *processes.* I could tell from his expression that Mr. Bodek didn't entirely understand what I meant.

This encounter made me realize that although I have discussed individual issues such as the Single-minute Exchange of Die (SMED) System, Zero Quality Control (ZQC), and the Nonstock Production System, I haven't yet talked about the mutual relationships among them. "Of course!" I thought. If I want to explain how to get from Osaka to Tokyo, all I have to do is say, "Follow the Meishin and Tōmei expressways." On the way there is another road, the Hokurikudō, that goes from Maibara to Kanazawa, and from Nagoya there is a road that goes toward Nagano and another, the Meihandō, that will take you to Osaka through Matsuzaka. "Wouldn't it be easier to grasp," I realized, "if I showed the *entire network* of roads at the same time?"

When we see a doctor, a complete physical examination checks both (1) the status of individual body functions and (2) the interrelationships among those functions. In doing so, it reveals unsuspected problems and can prompt early treatment of a number of conditions. The result is either that we correct hitherto unnoticed problems or that we are relieved to find that nothing is abnormal.

Similarly, it would be useful if we could submit current production functions and management practices to a comprehensive examination in order to find out the state of things. No doubt we would discover some things that had been overlooked and be relieved to learn that others were functioning normally.

Suppose we were to draw up a comprehensive map of production functions for the purposes of such an examination. What would these functions look like? I undertook to write the present book in an attempt to provide those engaged in production management with a constructive answer to that question.

As I began to write, I felt strongly that improvement *(kaizen)* was the key. But there are two points that should be stressed in discussing improvement:

1. People sometimes mistakenly believe intermediate-level improvements to be ultimate improvements. If they have raised to 80 percent what used to be at 50 percent, they tend to think of that as a limit and overlook the fact that it can be increased to 100 percent.
2. People are in the habit of thinking that an improvement affecting only one sector or department means the improvement of production overall. An excessive trust in the effects in that one department leads them to make exaggerated claims.

As the phrase implies, the "improvement of production management systems" involves understanding two things: (1) what a "production management system" is and (2) how to carry out improvement.

Why is it that the West never created concepts such as SMED, zero defects, source inspections and the *poka-yoke* system, and non-stock production? It seems to me that the answer is that the improvement-oriented ideas of F.B. Gilbreth have not always sunk in. With this in mind, I have devoted an entire chapter to explaining what I call the *Scientific Thinking Mechanism* (STM) for improvement and am especially anxious that readers study it carefully.

Much in this book repeats material appearing in my previous work, titled *Non-stock Production System: The Shingo System for Continuous Improvement* (Productivity Press, 1988). Even though the books were written for different purposes, they are both about the improvement of production management, and I hope readers will indulge my inevitable repetition.

My intention in writing the present volume has been to provide serious production managers and scholars with materials for study. Obviously, I cannot claim that the present book offers the last word. I earnestly hope, however, that others will revise and amend my thesis and that this book may therefore serve as a basis for the development of a more complete theory of production.

Part I

A History of
Production Management

> We go to the doctor for a complete physical examination in order to find out what condition our body is in. Why is it any less important to find out what the overall state of production management functions is?
>
> - What kind of functions are there?
> - What specific functions are called for?
> - How do those functions relate to each other?
> - How can we improve those functions?
>
> Has humankind forgotten that true production functions form a two-dimensional network of processes and operations? Have we neglected processes to look solely at operations?

1

Introduction

In 1988, I was awarded honorary degrees of Doctor of Management by two universities, Utah State University in the United States and the Université de Toulouse in France. Both institutions cited my work for "bringing revolutionary new developments to conventional assumptions about production functions." From the 1990s to the year 2000 and beyond, they said, basic thinking about production "will doubtless be led by Shigeo Shingo's Non-stock Production System, a system based on the recognition that *production is a network of processes and operations.*"

The realization that production is a network of processes and operations frees us of our obsession with streamlining operations and focuses our attention on making processes more rational. The result is unprecedented improvement. Now we can triple profits in the space of one year and increase them fivefold before two years are out. How?

- Lay the groundwork by using the SMED (Single-minute Exchange of Die) system to cut setup changeover times by 99 percent.
- Then make process-type improvements in machining or processing.
- Adopt a "Zero Defects" quality control system; i.e., use source inspections and the *poka-yoke* system (techniques of low-cost 100 percent inspections and immediate action). This eliminates defects by incorporating inspection into processing.

3

- Eliminate transport labor costs by using a layout system designed to reduce transport to zero.
- Use synchronized production and the full work system to eliminate process delays.
- Clearly recognize the lot delays that conventional Western production systems overlook. Use flow operations to eliminate lot delays, cut production cycles by 99 percent, and produce only after demand has been confirmed. These measures will reduce finished goods inventories to zero and, through the use of a one-piece flow system, eliminate delays between processes.
- Cut labor costs by 60 percent or more using these approaches to eliminate transport and delays.

The honorary Doctor of Management degree was awarded for creating and promoting these pioneering new production management ideas.

Photo 1-1. Honorary Doctoral Diploma Conferred by Utah State University

The Reaction at M.I.T.

In May 1989, I gave a lecture on the Shingo Non-stock Production System to a group of ten professors and 20 doctoral students at the Massachusetts Institute of Technology. When I asked for criticism of my theory of production management, the ranking professor, Dr. Alane, replied that he had no objection to what I had said.

> I used to teach that the most rational production would be achieved by (a) mechanizing and then automating human labor and then (b) increasing the operating rates of the machines to 100 percent. But you are telling us that machine operating rates can be low as long as total cost is low and profit is maximized. And machines should be built in-house at one-tenth of the market price.
>
> I used to think that operations, or tasks, constituted the only production functions. Now I see that production is a network composed of functions in two dimensions, processes and operations. I didn't understand the crucial function process plays in production. You've given me a lot to think about because I realize now that I've been teaching production management based on a theory that was wrong.

There can be little doubt that production management in the United States is on the threshold of a dramatic leap forward. American universities have already grasped these revolutionary new concepts in production management and they are applying these ideas in their teaching. Isn't it about time for Japan, too, to discard outmoded ideas and put valid production management concepts to work?

2
Historical Revolutions
in Production

THE DIVISION OF LABOR AND ITS FALLOUT

Understanding the historical course of production system revolutions throughout the world can be helpful in gaining an accurate grasp of the significance of current systems of production.

I think it is fair to say that the point of departure for production systems lies in the use of the division of labor in England in the 1750s. In his 1776 book, *The Wealth of Nations*, Adam Smith explains how even the most skilled craftsman was capable of making only twenty pins a day. When the idea of the division of labor was introduced, however, the process of pin fabrication was broken down into eighteen steps such as drawing, straightening, cutting, sharpening, grinding, and attaching the head. With those eighteen steps distributed among ten people, it was possible to produce 48,000 pins per day, or 4,800 pins per person. This is 240 times the number of pins an individual had been able to make previously.

Similarly, dividing the labor of needle production more than doubled output by allowing one person to produce 2,000 needles per day instead of the 800 to 1,000 needles the most skilled workers had been able to make by the conventional method.

The division of labor resulted in a dramatic decrease in the price of pins and expanded the demand for pins as new employment opportunities for unskilled workers increased salaries. In this way, the division of labor hastened the growth of British industry, which in turn led to national prosperity and more comfortable lives for individuals.

Industry flourished as the concept of the division of labor spread to other industries and then to other countries.

THE PROCESS/OPERATION DISTINCTION AND THE NEGLECT OF PROCESSES

When you have a situation in which operators work successively on the same parts A1, A2, A3 . . . , a single product A will be lengthened by operator P, straightened by operator Q, cut by operator R, and so forth. This clearly gives rise to the phenomenon of *process*, that is, a flow by which an object is transformed from raw material into finished product. Yet, people tend to concentrate solely on the operations they see when they stop and observe production, and for a long time process phenomena failed to attract much notice.

In fact, the problem was overlooked for a century and a half after Adam Smith's book until the American Frank B. Gilbreth published in the journal of the American Society of Mechanical Engineers his contention that production is composed of two phenomena, operations and processes. Despite this clear recognition of process phenomena, however, Gilbreth defined a process as a large unit for analyzing production and an operation as a small unit of analysis. His understanding, in other words, was that processes and operations were substantially similar analytical units differing only in scale. The result was that worldwide efforts to make production more rational focused on operations. Process improvements were largely neglected. Enhanced operability became the target of all production improvement. In the orthodox view, the use of tools would be followed by mechanization, then automation and robotization.

THE SCIENCE OF WORK

American managers in the 1880s accepted the idea that workers were basically lazy. They developed an incentive pay scheme, the piecework system, to stimulate workers to perform difficult jobs. Vague standards for tasks and times led to increased efficiency and cost reductions. However, worker enthusiasm

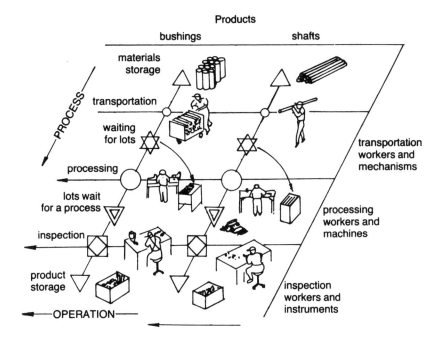

Figure 2-1. The Two Streams of Production

dropped sharply as well, and efficiency declined as organizational sloth and soldiering spread.

Around 1880, Frederick W. Taylor decided that the problem lay in a failure to set scientific work standards. He developed a system of time studies, examined the various factors that affect work, and experimented with the establishment of firm standards for tasks and times. He supported this effort with human engineering research into the nature of work and fatigue.

At about the same time, Gilbreth, with his wife Lillian, worked out his principles of the economy of motion. They went on to develop what they called the science of "motion economy," creating a basic conceptual framework for improving work by economizing motion. The main thrust of this argument was as follows:

1. Analyze work in detail.
2. Track down the goals of work by repeatedly asking *why?*

3. Recognize that a single end may be reached by multiple means.
4. Seek out the one best way of performing a given task.

As a matter of course, the ideas of Taylor and Gilbreth were responsible for substantial gains in productivity. Productivity also benefited from the division of labor, which multiplied and simplified tasks. The overall idea was to gain qualitative improvements in work by using the division of labor to divide tasks, or operations, and then relentlessly study each individual task. But the basic perception equating production with operations remained unchanged.

THE HAWTHORNE WORKS EXPERIMENT: TYPE-X AND TYPE-Y PEOPLE

The Hawthorne Works experiments conducted by George Elton Mayo and his colleagues in 1927 demonstrated the presence of two crucial factors in human work — method and motivation. The experiments, in fact, can be seen as an attempt to influence work motivation. Mayo and the others found that gradually raising the level of illumination increased productivity, but they also found that productivity would rise even if they gradually darkened the workplace.

Industrial engineers were at a loss to explain this phenomenon. From a psychological viewpoint, the employees, knowing their daily output would be made public, responded to the attention focused on them by working harder.

With the Hawthorne experiments, the concept of improvement could no longer be applied only to work methods. Significant attention had to be paid to work motivation as well, and a new emphasis was placed on *human nature*.

In 1960, Douglas McGregor, a professor of industrial management at the Massachusetts Institute of Technology, submitted a manuscript titled *The Human Side of Enterprise* to the American Society of Mechanical Engineers. In his work, McGregor proposed a Theory X-Theory Y dichotomy, in which human nature has two conflicting aspects: a Type-X impulse to work passively and a Type-Y impulse to work actively.

The Reaction to Type-X and Type-Y People

How have these two aspects of human nature been handled? To deal with Type-X people:

- Management uses a piecework system to encourage worker effort.
- Lazy workers are eliminated through frequent layoffs.
- Labor forms radical, adversarial unions and uses strikes to oppose management.
- Something resembling a class distinction arises between labor and management.

And how are Type-Y traits dealt with?

- Management uses daily or monthly wage systems.
- Management stabilizes employment by adopting lifetime employment.
- Labor forms cooperative company unions.
- Companies promote circle activities and companywide campaigns.

Figure 2-2 presents a breakdown of what I call the "feeling human being." An important point is that Type-X and Type-Y characteristics are present in all human beings. Some companies have concentrated merely on exploiting Type-Y characteristics through approaches such as "Management by Objective (MBO) or zero defects (ZD) campaigns. Finally, managers could only devise approaches like the Volvo System, which abolishes conveyor lines in a concession to Type-X characteristics. Why?

In historical terms, the absence of natural resources has made Japan's prosperity as a nation dependent chiefly on human labor. This has resulted in a natural tendency toward Type-Y characteristics in Japan — a tendency supported by lifetime employment and other mechanisms. By contrast, I think it fair to say that U.S. managers of the 1880s who decided that workers were basically lazy encouraged the Type-X nature of labor, with the result that conflict came to dominate labor-management relations.

Why haven't managers built harmonious human relations by adopting policies that change Type-X traits into Type-Y traits, and why isn't their failure seen as a basic problem of human social

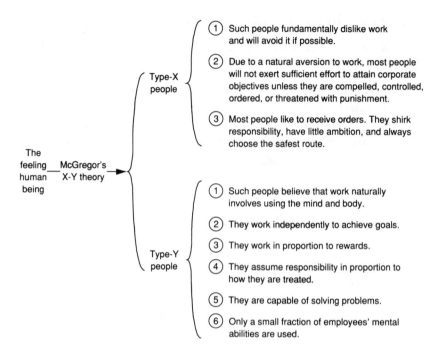

Figure 2-2. The Feeling Human Being

relationships? This is ultimately a problem that concerns work motivations. On the work methods side, there was still no change in the bias toward believing that production could be dealt with solely in terms of operations. Correcting this misperception is an issue of fundamental importance.

PRODUCTION IS A STRUCTURE IN TWO DIMENSIONS: PROCESSES AND OPERATIONS

As we have seen, the conventional approach to production improvement has been rooted in the mistaken notion that production is equivalent to operations. People have not realized that production is a network of processes and operations, a three-dimensional phenomenon in which processes (Y-axis) and operations (X-axis) change in accordance with flows of space and time (Z-axis) as shown in Figure 2-3.

The division of labor may have taught us about the existence of process phenomena, but an appreciation of this fact escaped humankind's notice for some two hundred years. It was in 1945 that I first dealt with processes on the same level as operations. The Toyota Production System was the first production system that logically integrated all aspects of production.

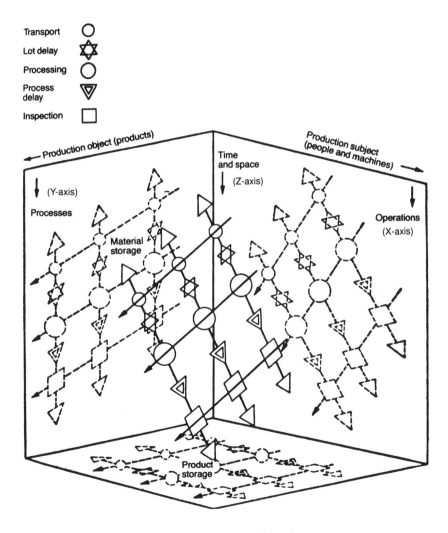

Figure 2-3. Three-dimensional Structure of Production

Toyota's production system was thrust abruptly into the spotlight of world attention at the time of the first oil shock of the 1970s when numerous other companies suffered considerable damage. Thus began the fashion of copying Toyota's *kanban* system and just-in-time (JIT) method — the superficial *know-how* of the Toyota system. It is important to go deeper and find a valid theory of production management. Companies must understand that this theory is embodied in a Non-stock Production System.

Understanding the Non-stock Production System requires a clear grasp of the fact that conventional production theories are based on principles skewed toward operations — not on a rational theoretical foundation that recognizes production to be a network of processes *and* operations. Obviously, no legitimate production system can develop if it is built on an erroneous foundation.

CORRECTLY UNDERSTANDING PROCESS PHENOMENA

I was conducting an improvement survey at Hitachi Ltd.'s Kudamatsu plant in 1945 when it dawned on me that production was a two-dimensional network of processes and operations. During the course of that survey, I asked a plant researcher to do an analysis of a piston rod process. He asked me whether a thirty-minute period in which piston rods had to wait for a crane constituted a process delay or a lot delay. I replied that since he was conducting his survey along the process flow, the thirty-minute wait should be considered a process delay.

"If you tell me the thirty minutes is a process delay, I'm willing to call it that," he said, "but should we be thinking of it as a temporary delay?"

For that question I had no answer.

An American production handbook uses the expressions "control storage" and "temporary storage" to refer to delays occurring between processes. In Japan, we have translated these terms as "process delay" and "temporary delay," respectively. As a result, the distinction between the two is widely thought to be one

Unit of Analysis and Analysis Method

Unit of Analysis	Job	Operation	Process	Collective Operation	Unit Operation	Elemental Operation	Elemental Motion	Therblig
Contents	Type K automobile production	Bolt A fabrication	Bolt A lathe machining	Thread cutting	Cutting-tool attachment	Grasp cutting tool	Reach for cutting tool	Search for cutting tool
Time-study means	Reporting or recording		Ordinary watch or reporting		Ordinary watch	Stopwatch	Collection of therbligs	Gilbreth watch/high-speed film
Method used	Rough process analysis		Process analysis	Unit-operation analysis		Elemental-operation analysis	Motion study	
Classification	← Process analysis →				← Operation analysis →			

Figure 2-4. Methods and Units of Analysis

of length of time. People assume that process delays are long periods of storage and temporary delays are short periods of storage. Indeed, this is the explanation given in an early Shōwa-era process textbook. Although the dividing line between the two is generally considered to be thirty minutes, the vagueness of a distinction based on length of time has led to much debate on the issue.

In actually analyzing what happens in the factory, however, I identified another, qualitatively different, type of delay.

Consider batch operations. In a lot of 1,000 pieces, 999 have to wait in an unprocessed state while the first piece is being processed. Similarly, 998 pieces wait while the second piece is being processed, and so on. Synchronizing all the pieces, moreover — assuring they all move together — means that the first completed piece doesn't move on to the next station until the entire lot has been processed. I gave the name "lot delays" to these delays caused by the running of a typical batch operation.

The storage of goods between processes should not be characterized by how long they wait (process delays versus temporary delays). Rather, a clear distinction should be drawn based on the nature of the delay: process delays versus lot delays.

It follows that no matter the timeframe, a delay that keeps the entire lot waiting is a process delay, and a delay for the purpose of synchronizing lot movement is a lot delay. Once we establish a clear meaning for these terms, arguments about what happens over or under thirty minutes become immaterial.

By looking at lot delays, we find we can substantially cut the time disparity between processes by reducing the size of transport lots between processes and by sending each piece on to the next process as soon as work at one process has been completed. This allows us to shorten the entire production cycle dramatically. In fact, a so-called "one-piece flow" production system enables us to cut production lead times to as much as a hundredth of what they used to be (see Figure 2-5).

- With batch, or lot, production, nT is the production cycle. If $T = 5$ hours and there are 10 processes ($n = 10$), the production cycle (L) = 50 hours.
- But if each piece coming out of one process flows immediately on to the next process, the production cycle (l) =

$T + (n - 1)t$, where t = processing time per piece (say 0.3 seconds). Thus:

$$l = 5 + (10 - 1) \times 0.3 \text{ seconds}$$
$$= 5 \text{ hours } 2.7 \text{ minutes}$$

And:

$$\frac{l}{L} = \frac{T + (n - 1)t}{nT} \approx \frac{1}{n} = \frac{5° - 2.7'}{50°} = \frac{302.7'}{3000} \approx \frac{1}{10}$$

Thus, since $(n - 1)$ is generally very small with respect to T, the production cycle can usually be shortened to one-nth of its original value.

The disadvantage of this approach is an increase in the number of transport trips. Where a single transportation run may suffice for a lot of 1,000 pieces, 1,000 trips have to be made if each piece is transported separately.

Two methods are used to address this problem:

1. Machines are laid out according to the process so workpieces move smoothly from one station to the next.
2. Workpieces are moved between physically separated machines using simple "one-piece" transport devices.

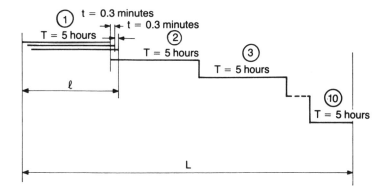

Figure 2-5. Lot Delay Reductions

When similar machines are grouped together and the equipment is difficult to move, it is often effective to install overhead transport devices to move pieces one at a time.

The concept of "lot delay" does not appear in the production handbook previously mentioned. Therefore, while some factories have stumbled onto the idea of using one-piece flow production, the practice actually has no theoretical basis. As a result, the concept appears to have been applied only partially and in restricted contexts. Both in Japan and in the West, the idea of using one-piece flow operations to eliminate lot delays will have an enormous impact on the development of new systems of production.

There are a number of deficiencies in conventional production management philosophy that we must discover and correct as soon as we can.

3

A Production Management Revolution in the United States

We can get a glimpse of the future of Japanese companies by learning how American companies are improving right now.

GRANVILLE-PHILLIPS

Dr. Daniel B. Bills, the Harvard-educated co-founder and president of Granville-Phillips Company, is an uncommon and perceptive man. The first time I visited him I noticed a large statistical chart hanging on the wall of his office. I asked him about the chart and he told me it was a statistical summary of the previous month's reject rates.

"Tear it down!" I replied. "Those statistics are nothing more than a death certificate. They're utterly meaningless. If you want to get rid of defects, why don't you go out to the shop floor right now and eliminate them from the operations that produce them?"

I had him take me out to the operation that was causing the most problems, a process in which the top of a product housing was soldered. The task consisted of fitting together two parts of the housing, placing a string of solder around the assembly, and then melting the solder with a gas burner.

The assembly contained a 50-millimeter printed circuit board covered by a heat-resistant cap to prevent excess heat from the burner from causing shorts on the board. Even so, the operation was generating rejects at a rate of 10.8 percent per month.

19

Photo 3-1. The author and Daniel Bills, president of Granville-Phillips Company.

As we observed the operation, I asked Dr. Bills what the process was for.

"It's for melting the solder and welding the two halves of the housing together," he replied.

"And what melts the solder?" I asked.

"The burner."

"Wrong," I said. "The burner does not melt the solder."

"All right," said Dr. Bills. "It's not the burner. The burner flame is melting it."

"Wrong again," I replied.

"In that case," Dr. Bills went on. "it's the heat of the burner flame."

"Right!" I exclaimed. "Now, if it's the heat you need, why not turn the flame so that it is tangential to the housing instead of aimed directly at it the way it is now?"

We immediately changed the position of the flame, one action that completely eliminated defects caused by circuit board shorts.

"You see," I told Dr. Bills, "work should never be without purpose. We need to ask ourselves constantly about the real function of work. What is the purpose of the task? We need to improve each task by asking '*Why?*' and then by finding a more suitable way to achieve that goal. Whenever we come across a problem, we need to ask the question '*Why?*' at least three times."

Not long afterward, I was told that Granville-Phillips had been able to cut its reject rates substantially because all of its employees had acquired the habit of asking "*Why?*" Of course, the statistical charts in Dr. Bills' office have vanished.

Dr. Bills is now a firm believer, and the results he reports are impressive:

- The old layout by machine type was converted to a process-based layout, and one-piece flows were instituted. Under the old batch production system, the lead time (production cycle) was four weeks. Now it is two hours.
- Application of the single-minute exchange of die (SMED) system has allowed setups that used to take two hours to be performed in two minutes. The plant now produces to firm orders in lots of 30 or so where it used to build products in large lots of 500 based on market projections. Finished goods inventories have dropped to zero.
- Establishing one-piece flow operations has both (1) eliminated the storage of parts between processes and (2) saved on transportation. Labor costs have dropped 60 percent as a result.
- Only half the floor space used previously is needed to build the product. The newly freed-up space is being used by the newly freed-up employees to begin manufacturing new products.

According to Dr. Bills, eliminating interprocess storage and finished goods inventories has resulted in:

1. tripled profits the first year
2. quintupled profits the second year
3. double the product development budget the third year

Although Granville-Phillips does not have an adversarial labor union, employees and management weekly meetings have produced the following results:

1. *Employees' wishes are expressed and heard.* If the company cannot respond immediately, management explains its constraints.
2. *New initiatives and programs that management wants developed are presented.* These are explained before implementation in order to gain the understanding and consent of employees. The programs are introduced only after any required corrections have been made.
3. *Base pay levels have been raised in response to managerial initiative.* Against this background, the company has performed at a consistently high level and strike-free for ten years.

UNITED ELECTRIC

United Electric Control Company, a U.S. process control manufacturer of some 300 employees, had been a strong candidate for the 1989 Shingo Prize. I visited United Electric in May of that year.

I was told the company wanted me to look at setup operations on an air press stamping machine at the back of the plant. I had hardly stepped onto the shop floor, however, when a crowd of employees on both sides of the aisle began applauding me. Their welcome stunned me and, in my wheelchair, I shook hands with about a hundred people.

Later I had my hosts show me the stamping machine and I advised them on how to make the setup more rational. Not only were shop floor managers and workers enthusiastically receptive to what I told them, they also made a number of spontaneous suggestions of their own. When it was time to go, I found many employees waiting to shake my hand again.

At this point, I asked company president Dave Reis and his brother Bob Reis, who is chairman of the board, whether they had orchestrated this welcome for me.

"Absolutely not!" was their reply. "The employees did it themselves. Actually, our father is a big fan of yours, and many employees have read your books."

They went on to explain that at the end of a two-year companywide improvement effort, productivity had tripled. Other results were:

- Work-in-process and product lead times were reduced by 90 percent.
- Total plant inventory dropped 70 percent and stockrooms were eliminated.
- Cash generated through improvements to existing production lines fueled the acquisition of two companies with compatible instrumentation, greatly enhancing the company's market position.
- Through the use of worker-generated *poka-yoke* devices, in-process inspections were cut by 85 percent.
- Three manufacturing facilities were consolidated to one despite increasing sales volume.
- Employee participation in continuous improvement rose from 5 percent to 90 percent in just three years.

GLOBE ALLOY METAL

Globe Alloy Metal is an alloy manufacturer with approximately 150 employees. It was awarded the 1990 Shigeo Shingo Prize for having best understood and implemented Japanese production management techniques.

Until fairly recently, extremely poor productivity and high defect rates had led investors to announce they would either sell off the company or dissolve it. Employee morale was low, and the plant manager felt a sense of impending doom.

In October 1987, however, he happened to attend a Productivity, Inc., conference in San Francisco. There, he was startled to hear me tell about the SMED system that can reduce setup changeover times from four hours to three minutes and about the many Japanese companies that were using "one-touch" changeovers that take less than one minute. I also talked about the "Zero Quality Control" system, a system of source inspections and mistake-proof *poka-yoke* devices, and about the Non-stock Production System.

Impressed by what he had heard, he bought thirty copies of my books and went back to form a working group with his managers. By December 1988, the aggressive improvements they made resulted in:

- doubled productivity
- the virtual disappearance of defects
- a 90 percent reduction in inventories

Orders, which previously had amounted to only 60 percent of plant capacity, grew to 130 percent, and management voluntarily raised employee wages by 30 percent. Employee morale soared as profitability returned and improvement activities continued. The Shingo Prize was awarded in recognition of this dramatic turnaround in performance.

A REVOLUTION IN U.S. PRODUCTION MANAGEMENT THEORY

American companies and universities are recognizing and correctly using my "true theory of production management." *Modern Approaches to Manufacturing Improvement: The Shingo System*, a digest of my ideas edited by Dr. Alan Robinson of the University of Massachusetts at Amherst, is used as a textbook at many U.S. universities. In addition, the number of companies actually practicing those ideas is increasing. I think we can expect a major revolution to take place in the next few years in the United States.

That revolution will take us beyond the conventional focus on improving operations. It will spring from the realization that production is a network of operations and processes and from a proper grasp of the fact that process improvements should receive priority over operational improvements.

In contrast, Japanese academic circles and many Japanese companies are still hostage to production theories that U.S. universities have discarded. Indeed, it may not be too long before Japan will have to target the United States with sanctions against "unfair" trade practices.

Although still in its early stages, a revolution in production management is already taking place in the United States. Japan must not be allowed to fall behind.

Part II

Basic Improvement Thinking

4

The Concept of Improvement

In this chapter we discuss the fundamental kind of thinking needed for improving production management.

We will see Gilbreth's concepts mark the point of departure for improvement.

GILBRETH AND THE "MOTION ECONOMY" CONCEPT

In both Japan and the West, I am sometimes asked what secret techniques I use for creating ideas such as SMED, source inspections and the mistake-proof *poka-yoke* system, or the Non-stock Production System. I always reply the same way.

The man who taught me about improvement was Kenichi Horigame, a former managing director of the Japan Management Association (JMA). His teacher was Engineering Lieutenant Jirō Kakuda of the Yokosuka Navy Yard, who learned about improvement from Frank B. Gilbreth. Dr. Horigome greatly admired Gilbreth's philosophy and gave me a thorough training in Gilbreth's concept of "motion economy." At a two-month production engineering seminar held at the Unozawa Steel Works in Tokyo in 1937, for example, I spent days doing motion studies and proposing various improvements. I had Gilbreth's basic concepts drilled into me:

1. When faced with a problem, seek out goals by relentlessly asking "*Why?*"
2. Keep an open mind — there are many means to any end. Think freely and don't be imprisoned by orthodox ideas.
3. Always look for the *best single way.*

What these lessons boiled down to for me was seeking out purposes and goals by repeatedly asking "*Why?*"

I learned to look for flaws in what I had always accepted as standard methods. When trying to identify ideas for improvement, I learned to try out proposals and not reject them out of hand. Naturally, there were ideas I wanted to discard right away. In some cases, however, I was able to use them successfully by asking *why* they couldn't possibly work.

Maybe I have come up with some original ideas because I have asked "*why?*" more than other people have. Improvement demands (1) repeatedly asking "*why?*" and (2) a stubborn refusal to give up. I am greatly indebted to Dr. Horigome and am, of course, a steadfast believer in Gilbreth.

5

A Scientific Thinking Mechanism for Improvement

Anybody hoping to improve must understand the Scientific Thinking Mechanism (STM) for improvement that I developed as an extension of Gilbreth's ideas.

While Gilbreth may have taught us the essential concept of improvement, many specific factors influence improvement on the shop floor. It seems necessary to me to consider those factors systematically. This is what led me to create a "Scientific Thinking Mechanism" (STM) for improvement. It is illustrated in Figure 5-1.

WHAT ARE PRINCIPLES OF CLASSIFICATION?

First, it is important to have a clear understanding of principles of classification. A principle of classification — what logicians refer to as a *fundamentum divisionis*, or principle of division — is a basic idea that allows us to distinguish one thing from another. Most things can be distinguished either through classification by opposition or through continuous classification.

In classification by opposition, something is clearly either *A* or not *A*. Anyone can distinguish between *man* and *woman*, for example, using the classificatory principle of sex or gender.

In continuous classification, however, the classificatory principle is gradual. For example, age is a continuous phenomenon that does not lend itself to objective judgment in distinguishing between a child and an adult. The only way we can determine the

31

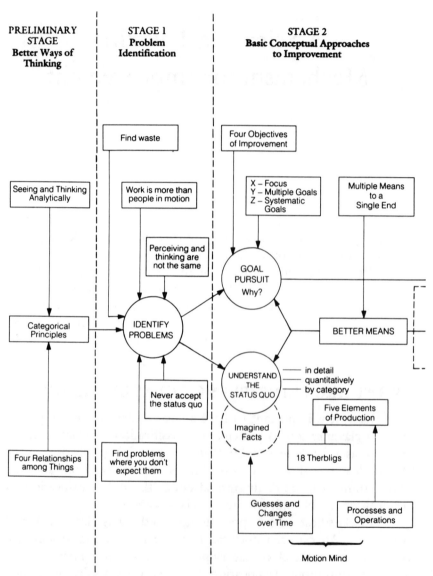

Figure 5-1. Scientific Thinking Mechanism for Improvement

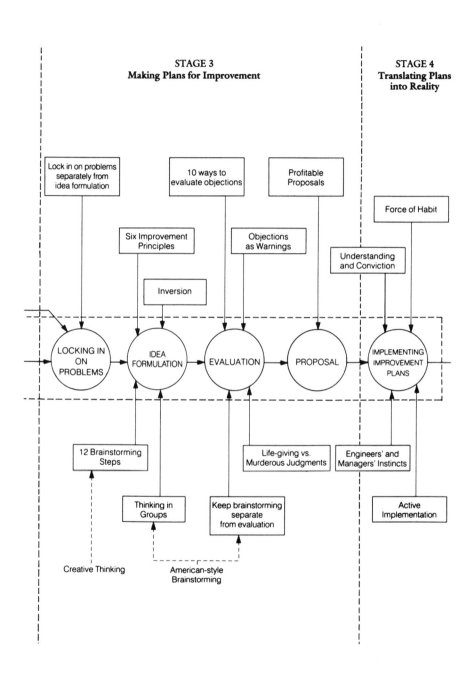

dividing line between the two is to have everyone express his or her own opinion and then take the rounded-off average of those judgments. In other words, we have to make judgments the same way gymnastics events are scored in the Olympics: each judge gives a score and all the scores are averaged. This kind of evaluation is inherently subjective and cannot be resolved by discussion.

In response to Japan's recently imposed sales (or "consumption") tax, many people have demanded that the law be amended to exempt fresh foodstuffs. Were such a change to be made, all fresh foods would be tax-exempt. Some people apparently object to the proposed change, saying that *matsutake* mushrooms, for example, cost $6.66 apiece. Obviously, however, if you exempt fresh foods there should be no exceptions. If we cannot get used to the idea of exempting exceptionally high-priced vegetables, we should consider using a per-unit price limit as a secondary principle of classification. Price, of course, is a continuous phenomenon, and we would have to use the Olympic scoring approach to determine a cutoff point.

Nevertheless, we should not be confused by short-sighted arguments. The approach taken should lead to a higher political goal. The government wants to cut direct taxation and use a sales tax to apportion the burden to all citizens. This will promote a more equitable sharing of that burden as long as separate relief measures are provided for those with low incomes, measures that will also make the package easier to sell to taxpayers.

Another difficult problem is posed by "cross divisions," or *intersecting* principles of classification. Fresh foodstuffs are a necessity, so let's say we make them tax-exempt. However, because we do not want to exempt luxury goods, we use two criteria to classify items: (1) the nature of the product and (2) the per-unit price. This gives us the following distinctions:

1. fresh foodstuffs versus other items
2. items with high unitary prices versus those with low unitary prices

Applying two classificatory principles at the same time yields an intersecting classification that cannot be broken down further. The first classificatory principle divides items on the basis of inherent characteristics; a second, subordinate principle classifies them by price. We should note two points here. First, the subordinate principle in our example must be applied incrementally. Second, it is crucial never to lose sight of the higher goal of the division. Sometimes we tend to get so wrapped up in debate over methods of classification that we forget the original purpose.

FIND *MUDA*! FIND WASTE!

I once gave a talk in an industrial zone of Osaka to people from about 80 firms affiliated with Company A. I remarked to Mr. K, the president of the host company, that all the people in his firm were idiots.

"What do you mean?" he replied indignantly. "I'm not one to boast, but they're all top-notch people!"

"If that's the case, then why do you have the slogan '*Get Rid of Waste!*' framed and hanging on your office wall?" I asked. "I assume it must be because your people know where waste is but they don't do anything about getting rid of it."

Mr. K was silent.

"Once waste is identified, everybody wants to get rid of it," I went on. "So shouldn't your slogan be '*Find Waste!*' instead?"

We sometimes hear about worker dissatisfaction and complaints, but it is a mistake to equate one with the other — especially when improvement begins with dissatisfaction. Improvement never happens when people are satisfied with the way things are. Dissatisfaction is important, but the problem is that some people tend to convert dissatisfactions into complaints and to list reasons why things can't be changed. They say their bosses are not interested, or there is no room in the budget, or it is too much trouble to make improvements. The opposite, however, is needed. We need to go out of our way to link each thing we do to improvement.

In any event, the trick is to find waste, or *muda*. We need to question the status quo by constantly asking "*why?*" — even when we aren't aware of any problems. After all, the most damaging kind of waste is the waste we don't recognize.

THE FIVE ELEMENTS OF PRODUCTION

In Japan the expression "5W1H" often comes up when talking about perceiving facts. As illustrated in Figure 5-2, the acronym stands for:

1. What? (object)
2. Who? (subject)
3. How? (method)
4. Where? (space)
5. When? (time)
6. Why?

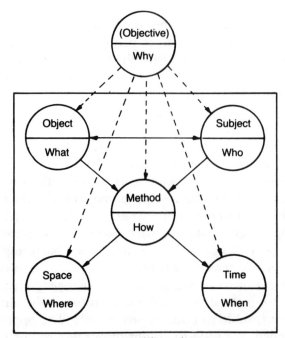

Elements comprising a phenomenon

Figure 5-2. Five Elements of Production: 5W1H

Let's look at each of these questions as it applies to production.

WHAT *Is to Be Produced? (Object of Production)*

Value engineering (VE) and similar studies show that production methods may vary considerably in response to changes in the nature or shape of the product to be made.

WHO? *(Subject of Production)*

Even when a decision has been made as to what will be manufactured, there may be several "whos" — people or machines — capable of making it. This question addresses the *means* of production, in other words. Changes in the *who* can directly affect overall production.

In the past, production improvement — that is, operational improvement — centered on this question.

HOW? *(Operational Methods)*

Both process and operations aspects of production must be considered when answering the question "what methods do we use?" The conventional tendency has been to put undue emphasis on operational aspects. Not only that, but of these two kinds of operations, (1) primary operations (actual machining) and (2) incidental operations (loading and unloading workpieces), conventional improvement efforts have concentrated on incidental operations. Just as Taylor's studies resulted in his discovery of an alloy and heat treatment that created "high-speed steel" (which could be made into cutting tools that would not soften at red heat), we need to put more energy into the study of specific technologies.

There has been much talk about superconductivity recently. Let's look at it from this *how* perspective. In evolutionary terms, mechanization enhanced the power of the human hand, and electricity was used as a means of transmitting that power. Superconductivity is extremely effective in reducing energy losses during the transmission of electricity. Production requires a supply of energy — and electricity has shown itself to be effective in transmitting that energy. Yet, isn't superconductivity being viewed merely as a means of streamlining incidental operations? In any case, the question of methods can have a tremendous impact on the shape of production.

WHERE? *(Space)*

This question influences and requires improvement in two aspects of transportation: (1) transport itself (how should machines be laid out?) and (2) transport operations (how should transport operations be set up once the layout is determined?). We might refer to these two aspects as transport from a process perspective and transport from an operations perspective.

Transport is fundamentally an activity that generates no added value. Therefore, we need to think first about eliminating transport by improving layout. Many people think only of streamlining transport operations — and this is a mistake. We need to do our utmost to reduce transport itself to zero.

WHEN? *(Time)*

The two questions we need to consider here are duration and timing.

In production, the question *"when?"* sometimes expresses the disadvantage of having inventories on hand. It may also come up in describing two types of delays: (1) process delays (delays between processes) and (2) lot delays (delays in which individual pieces wait to move with the entire batch). These delays are critical in defining two types of production systems:

- the Authorized Production System (ASP), in which stocks are tolerated, and
- the Non-stock Production System (NSP).

In the past, people have referred to stock as "a necessary evil." Conceding it to be an evil, however, they emphasize it as necessary and inevitable. Indeed, this sort of fuzzy thinking is one of the great weaknesses of European and U.S. production management.

The word "delay" is used in the narrow sense of a temporal phenomenon, while the terms "storage" or "stock" are used to designate the corresponding quantitative phenomenon. However, both types of phenomena lengthen lead times and significantly lower the value added in production.

IDENTIFYING PROCESS DELAYS AND LOT DELAYS

Western books discuss two kinds of delays: control delays (delays allowed for in the production plan) and temporary delays (such as unexpected delays caused by the late arrival of materials or machine breakdowns). In Japan these terms have been translated as process delays *(kō teimachi)* and temporary delays *(ichijimachi)*, respectively. The distinction between them (usually put at thirty minutes) is widely believed to be one of duration.

In the course of doing a 1945 survey of Hitachi Ltd., one researcher from the company questioned me about his analysis of a piston rod process. He told me the piston rod had waited about 30 minutes for a crane to arrive and asked me whether that was a "process delay" or a "crane delay." The question startled me, and I told him to record it as a process delay since he was analyzing a process.

Not entirely satisfied, however, I discussed the question with a colleague from the Japan Management Association. Even so, we couldn't come to a clear conclusion. The problem remained in my mind, and after a month of pondering, it occurred to me that the distinction between process delays and temporary delays was not one of duration. A *process delay* occurs when an entire lot has to wait for the previous lot to be processed, regardless of the length of time. On the other hand, a *lot delay* occurs when parts wait in order to synchronize their movement with the lot to which they belong. In a lot of 1,000 pieces, for example, 999 unfinished pieces wait while the first piece is being processed and 998 pieces wait while the second piece is in the machine. At the same time, the first piece waits in the processed state.

It finally dawned on me that lot delays are inherently different from process delays and that the distinction has nothing to do with the length of the delay. This was the point at which I hit on the idea for a "one-piece flow," because transporting pieces in lots of one to the next process is the only way to eliminate lot delays.

The absence of the concept of lot delays in Europe and the United States means that many companies that use one-piece flows have simply stumbled onto the method by accident. According to

Charles E. Sorensen, the originator of Ford's flow system, there are too many parts if assembly is carried out at one fixed location. Productivity can be improved significantly, he wrote, by dividing up the assembly process and arranging parts at each station. This seems, however, to have been no more than an operational improvement. And while Ford may have adopted "one-car flow" operations in its assembly process, its press shops didn't always use one-piece flow methods.

ELIMINATING LOT DELAYS

As discussed previously, no clear notion of lot delay seems to have developed in Europe or the United States. The production handbook devotes twenty-one pages to a discussion of process delays and not a single page to lot delays.

In stating that production is a network of processes and operations, I explained that there were two different kinds of delays, process delays and lot delays. This was the first time full recognition was conferred on the concept of lot delay — and with it came a clear understanding of the nature of one-piece flow operations.

One-piece flow operations have undoubtedly been dramatically effective in shortening production lead times. Also, they vastly increase the number of transportation runs between processes. While conventional batch operations may require a single transportation run for a lot of 1,000 pieces, a one-piece flow means 1,000 transport runs.

This is why it is so effective to adopt a process-based layout and to use chutes and other inexpensive devices to transport items simply and automatically from one process to the next. In the real world, one unavoidably encounters situations where the high cost of altering current layouts demands the installation of inexpensive but effective transport mechanisms between processes. In many instances, such supplementary measures have proved very effective in improving efficiency.

To summarize, using the "Five Elements of Production" as a guide to examining the status quo enables us to grasp the situation comprehensively and without dangerous oversights.

WHY? THE PURSUIT OF GOALS

The five elements of production (5W1H) just discussed cover the elements that make up the status quo. If we want to improve the present situation, we must direct the question "*why?*" at each of those elements repeatedly and relentlessly:

1. *Why* do we need this object?
2. *Why* do we require this subject?
3. *Why* use this kind of method?
4. *Why* this kind of space?
5. *Why* this kind of time?

Moreover, we need to consider the situation from all three aspects (X, Y, and Z) by conducting a thorough pursuit of goals or purposes in three dimensions.

A GRASP OF THE FACTS AND THE RELENTLESS PURSUIT OF GOALS

Grasping the Facts

Getting the facts is the first step toward improvement. It turns out that, rather than looking at the facts, people often have a "feel" for them based on supposition. They confuse guesswork for fact. In many cases, people misread the facts because facts are subject to diachronic change — that is, change over time — or because it is too much trouble to go out and verify facts on the shop floor.

We often talk about how something should be when we are merely guessing at the facts. Facts frequently turn out to be different from our guesses. One essential prerequisite of improvement is that we trade in "should be" for "is." Observations by which we gain a clear grasp of the facts must be

- *detailed* (for example, we should use "therbligs" or motion elements);
- *quantitative* (we should avoid vague terms such as "about," "approximately" or "various"); and

• *discriminating* (principles of classification should not be ambiguous).

It is effective at this point to use the techniques of motion analysis devised by Frank B. Gilbreth as shown in Figure 5-3.

Pursuing Goals: Why? What for?

In the improvement process, Gilbreth emphasizes the importance of seeking out goals. He asks: Why? Why? Why? And while he is perfectly right, he is too abstract. I think a more concrete explanation is desired. Therefore, my Scientific Thinking Mechanism (STM) divides the pursuit of goals into three parts:

• X — focus
• Y — identify multiple goals
• Z — pursue goals systematically

Focusing (X) is the idea of uncovering goals that are deeper than the immediately obvious ones. One example of focusing comes from a company called Koga Kinzoku Kōgyō. A planer had already been provided with a quick-return mechanism to minimize the time wasted while tools "cut the air" as they returned to the ready position. Koga's president, Yukio Koga, went further and wondered why the machine couldn't cut on the return half of the cycle as well. By turning the cutting tool 180° at the end of the outbound cut, the machine was able to cut in both directions. The resulting cutting efficiency increased by 85 percent.

Identifying multiple goals (Y) is the idea behind an improvement in the spraying of Teflon onto a household iron. Spraying both the bottom and the sides of an iron used to require two separate operations. By installing a stopper at the end of one pass, however, it is now possible to spray both the bottom and sides of the iron because the nozzle automatically shifts from a right-hand to a left-hand oblique position when the nozzle and stopper come in contact.

Pursuing goals systematically (Z) refers to the idea of looking at current goals from a broader perspective. This mode of goal pursuit may be seen in an example from Hiroshi Kondō, managing director of San'ei Kinzoku Kōgyō in Kyūshū. At San'ei, concern

Therbligs

Class	No.	Name	Symbol	Description
1	1	Assemble	⌗	Shape of combined rods
	2	Disassemble	⧺	One rod removed from a combined shape
	3	Deform (use)	U	U for "use," or a cup placed upright
2	4	Transport empty (extending or retracting your hand)	⏝	Shape of palm opened up
	5	Grab	∩	Shape of hand grabbing
	6	Transport	⌣	Shape of object being transported with hand
	7	Release	⌢	Shape of object with hand facing down
3	8	Search	⊙	Symbol of searching eye
	9	Find	⊙	Symbol of eye having located object after search
	10	Select	→	Symbol of finger pointing at selected object
	11	Inspect	0	Shape of a lens
	12	Regrasp (reposition)	9	Symbol of regrasping object held by finger tips
	13	Hold	⨅	Shape of rod held with hand
	14*	Prepare	8	Shape of a cuestick standing erect
4	15*	Think	⅌	Shape of a thinking person with hand by head
	16*	Rest	℔	Shape of a person sitting on chair
	17	Unavoidable delay	⌢o	Shape of tripped person on ground
	18*	Avoidable delay	∟o	Shape of person lying down

Note: An asterisk indicates a therblig that does not usually arise during normal tasks.

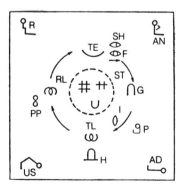

Figure 5-3. Four Classes of Motion

with how quickly burrs could be removed was replaced by efforts to prevent burrs from occurring in the first place. The company began cutting in two steps — from above and below. Since burrs are generated where the tool leaves the material and not where it enters, this eliminated burrs completely.

The systematic pursuit of goals addresses perspectives that we tend to overlook and leads to spectacular improvements. Don't neglect this mode of goal pursuit.

The Convertibility of Goals and Means

As we can see in Figure 5-4, all worldly phenomena are related to one another in chains of means and goals (or ends).

1. When we are hungry, we eat. If this were all there were to it, it would not matter if what we ate were decayed or devoid of nutritional value.
2. Eating when we are hungry is only a means of serving the higher goal of obtaining nourishment.
3. Obtaining nourishment is only a means to the still higher goal of sustaining life.
4. And we must see sustaining life as simply a means to an even higher goal — an awareness of the meaning of life.

The appropriate means a particular individual chooses will be determined by the level of goal he or she recognizes. All too often, we mistake intermediate goals for ultimate goals and satisfy ourselves at that level. Figure 5-5 shows a sequence of operations as a series of goals and means. In another instance where metal was seizing, the addition of oil may have resolved the problem temporarily — but the part was likely to seize again. Instead, repeatedly asking the question *"why?"* led to the installation of a wire mesh strainer that eliminated the seizing problem forever.

1. Why does the metal seize? *Because it runs out of oil.*
2. Why does it run out of oil? *Because the oil line clogs up.*
3. Why does the oil line clog up? *Because chips build up in the oil.*
4. Why do chips build up in the oil? *Because there is no strainer.*

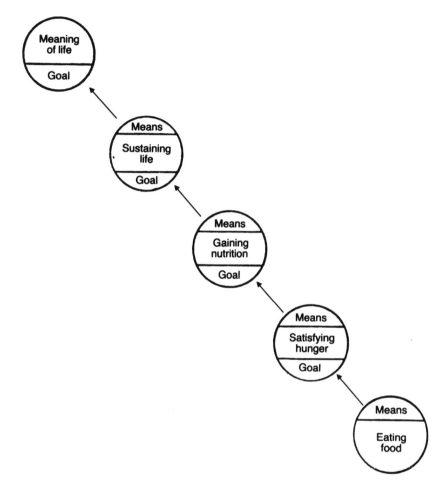

Figure 5-4. Convertibility of Means and Goals

It is crucial to pin down root causes this way and then take corrective action.

Many Means to a Single Goal

No matter how exhaustively a goal is pursued, improvement would be impossible if there were only one means associated with that goal.

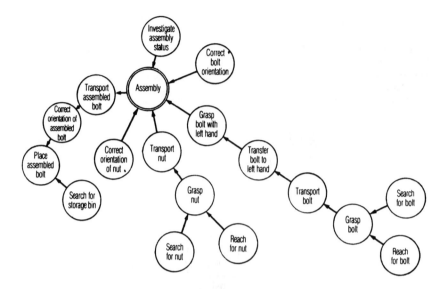

Figure 5-5. Series of Goals and Means

When I propose some modification of function on the shop floor, I often run up against the claim that what I have suggested is impossible with the current equipment. Yet, all I have suggested is that some shortcoming in the equipment be corrected. If short-comings in equipment cannot be corrected, improvement will never be possible.

We must learn to accept suggestions with an open mind and to take positive steps forward. The issue here boils down to the fact that effective measures depend on how fast we can come up with equipment with high investment ratios without making further investments.

Three Types of Engineers Who Hold Up Improvement

I often explain that in Japan there are three type of engineers who get in the way of improvement.

The first type are "table engineers" — people who enthusiastically debate around the conference table but never go onto the shop floor and dirty their hands by doing anything themselves. The loudest engineer wins the debate and has his or her plans implemented. However, things never turn out very well.

The second type are "catalogue engineers." When a new piece of equipment is needed, these engineers collect catalogues and propose the machines that look best to them. Their ideas, however, are never their own. Likewise, the machines they buy are inevitably equipped with extraneous functions that are designed to meet the demands of a wide range of companies. Ordinarily, suitable equipment can be constructed in-house at one-third to one-fifth the cost of these market machines because the outside vendor breaks down the sales price into three equal parts:

- idea fees and design costs
- actual manufacturing costs
- profit and the cost of rework risk, etc.

Manufacturing the same equipment in-house would entail only actual manufacturing costs. In addition, the people who designed and built it would be on hand to make rapid repairs should any problems arise.

In-house construction need not involve producing every equipment part in one's own factory. Significant cost reductions can be obtained simply by having subcontractors build parts and by doing as much of the assembly work as possible. Figure 5-6 considers this improvement method.

Lastly comes the third and most dangerous type of engineers — the "*nyet* engineers." This type recalls the days when Andrei Gromyko, then Soviet Ambassador to the United Nations, was nicknamed "Mr. Nyet" because he resoundingly vetoed all Western proposals.

Answering all proposals with a *nyet* no doubt precludes any improvement at all. No improvement can take place unless we keep an open mind and a positive attitude. And most important of all is a readiness to try any possible improvement.

Understanding the basic techniques of how improvement should be carried out lies at the heart of production management improvement.

(O : in-house fabrication   ✳ : subcontracted)

Job \ Step	A	B	C		D	E	F
Idea	O	O	O		O	O	✳
Design	O	O	✳		✳	✳	✳
Parts fabrication	O	✳	✳		✳	✳	✳
Assembly	O	O	O		✳	✳	✳
Maintenance	O	O	O		O	✳	✳
Risk	none	none	none		yes	yes	yes
Profit	none	small	small		large	large	large
Cost	10	20	30		60	80	100

✳ Consider what mechanisms are truly necessary. Eliminate superfluous mechanisms and create simple, inexpensive machines.

✳ Use "know-why" instead of "know-how" to fabricate the machine.

Figure 5-6. Stages of In-house Machine Construction

6

Creating an Improvement Plan

In this chapter we will examine specific tools for putting together an improvement plan.

The creation of an improvement plan requires taking the following five steps:

1. Observation	("That's odd!")
2. Idea formulation	("How about trying this?")
3. Judgment	("The idea is a little flawed in this respect....")
4. Suggestion	("But it can be implemented if we make this revision!")
5. Implementation	("Let's do it!")

Observation

Observation, or what we might call "locking in on the problem," means being dissatisfied with the way things are now and then making some judgment. Idea formulation involves providing answers to some doubt raised by observation. Observation precedes idea formulation — indeed, without observation there would be no improvement. In this sense, I suppose, observation is the mother of improvement.

Observation should be carried out in a purely critical spirit. Idea formulation should not be allowed to intrude at this point because it provides answers and has the effect of weakening critical thought.

At this stage, we can use A.F. Osborne's brainstorming techniques to generate as many observations as possible, freely and independently. In the ordinary course of events, we should be able to make roughly 1,000 observations about a three-minute operation.

Idea Formulation

Idea formulation generates ideas to address the points raised by observation and, therefore, constitutes the core of an improvement plan. Various techniques should be marshalled to generate ideas, including associative thinking and the input-output method.

I repeat that idea formulation should never be conducted simultaneously with observation. Nor should judgments ever be carried out at the idea formulation stage.

Judgment

After generating ideas, we use judgment to identify the shortcomings of our ideas. Some aspects of our ideas may be unrealistic or inadequate in some way. Making judgments at the same time that ideas are conceived ends up stifling ideas and suppressing the vitality of the idea generation process. It is more important than in the case of observation not to make judgments during idea generation. Osborne's brainstorming methods are very effective at this stage.

Suggestion

At this stage, ideas that have passed the judgment process are actually proposed.

Implementation

The finest improvement plan in the world is utterly worthless unless it is implemented. At this point, we must remember that, when the logic of an idea is explained to them, people will understand — but that understanding is no guarantee that the idea will be implemented. Only when they are persuaded by the idea will people put it into action.

Understanding is a function of the rational mind. On the other hand, persuasion depends on the emotions. In order to actually have someone implement an idea, you must convince both sides of a person: the rational side and the emotional side. Dale Carnegie's books on persuasion teach suitable approaches to take at this point.

(For further reading in this area, the editor recommends A.F. Osborne's *Applied Imagination* [New York: Scribner's/ MacMillan, 1963] plus the following books from Productivity Press [Cambridge, MA]: Japan Human Relations Association's *The Idea Book: Improvement through Total Employee Involvement* [1988]; Tomo Sugiyama's *The Improvement Book: Creating the Problem-free Workplace* [1989]; Michel Greif's *The Visual Factory* [1991]; Yuzo Yasuda's *40 Years, 20 Million Ideas: The Toyota Suggestion System* [1991]; John Psarouthakis's *Better Makes Us Best* [1989]; Ryuji Fukuda's *CEDAC: A Tool for Continuous Systematic Improvement* [1990]; and Will Kaydos's *Measuring, Managing, and Maximizing Performance* [1991].)

7

Basic Flaws in Conventional Production Management Improvement

One thing we need to realize is that numerous deficiencies in conventional systems of production management have long been overlooked. Why is it, we may wonder, that business executives, managers, and — most of all — scholars have made no move to correct serious and significant flaws in conventional production management? Production management founded on inadequate theory cannot be expected to show real development.

Improvement is misunderstood as well. Insufficient awareness leads many people to treat intermediate-level improvements as though they were ultimate improvements. Others are under the delusion that improvements limited to one sector of production are the same as improvements of production as a whole. Arguments that betray such misperceptions are common.

NEGLECT OF THE DIVISION OF LABOR AND PROCESS FUNCTIONS VERSUS THE TOYOTA PRODUCTION SYSTEM

As mentioned earlier, the mid-eighteenth-century development in England of the division of labor was an event that brought about an unprecedented increase in human productivity. Up until that time, the most skilled craftsperson working as hard as possible could only produce twenty pins a day. By contrast, a 200-fold increase in production was recorded when the process of pin manufacture was divided into eighteen distinct tasks (such as straightening the raw material, cutting the material, sharpening the tip, and grinding the tip).

This resulted in a considerable drop in the price of pins. It also made it possible for unskilled workers who previously had been unable to participate in industry to perform tasks and receive wages. Demand increased because these people were now able to buy pins. This effect snowballed to other items and sparked significant growth in British industry. This is the story detailed by Adam Smith in his 1778 book *The Wealth of Nations.*

The secret of the high productivity brought about by the division of labor probably lay in the fact that simplified tasks made individual judgments unnecessary. Also, the elimination of intermediate motions enabled work to be performed reflexively.

The concept of the division of labor spread throughout the world and contributed enormously to the growth of world industry. Until the Industrial Revolution, *process* (the flow from raw material to finished product) and *operation* (the flow of tasks performed by human workers on products) had been fused in the work of single individuals. One consequence of the division of labor was to separate processes from operations. The concept of process, however, was completely neglected in the mistaken belief that production was synonymous with operations.

Suppose worker A straightens out a length of raw material, worker B cuts it, worker C sharpens it, worker D grinds it, and so forth. This is clearly an example of a process — of the flow from raw material to finished product. Secondarily, the process is supplemented by other functions: worker A straightens out the first length of raw material, straightens out the second length of raw material, straightens out the third length of raw material, and so on. Worker B, in turn, carries out the operation of cutting each length of raw material in succession. Thus, an operation occurs when a human worker performs work on a product.

Therefore, the process represents a frontal view of the work. Operations fulfill a function secondary to that process.

PROCESSES AND OPERATIONS

The situation we have just described applies to all work: first process and then operations. While processes flow through the plant, however, an operation is performed in one spot and involves actually shaping the product. This is why we are more aware of operations and why process functions and phenomena end up escaping our attention. The result has been the delusion that production is synonymous with operations.

While the advent of the division of labor clearly separated processes and operations, this fact utterly escaped notice for some 170 years. It wasn't until 1921 that Frank B. Gilbreth reported to the American Society of Mechanical Engineers (1) that production included process phenomena and (2) that processes were composed of processing, inspection, transport and delay, or storage.

Gilbreth, however, committed a major error. He claimed that processes were phenomena identified by analyzing production in large units and that operations corresponded to small units of analysis. In other words, he saw processes and operations as phenomena lying on the same axis — phenomena that differed only in size of analytical unit. Despite his acknowledgment of process phenomena, this error once again led process functions to be buried in operations functions.

Following close observation of production activities, I first made the claim in 1945 that production was a network of processes and operations. I argued that processes and operations were clearly different production functions and felt that processes should command our primary attention when we look at production. Operations constitute second-order functions that supplement process functions. For the first time in the 215 years since the division of labor had separated processes and operations, then, I was making a clear argument for the independence of the process function.

In the Toyota production engineering seminars I have given to some 6,000 participants since 1955, I have emphasized a theory of production management rooted in the assertion that production is a network of processes and functions. Indeed, it is probably fair to say that this is the basis of Taiichi Ohno's Toyota Production System, a system that arguably is the first in the world to place major emphasis on process functions.

When repeated oil shocks inflicted serious damage on numerous companies, the extraordinary resiliency of the Toyota Production System brought it quickly to the attention of industrial circles around the world. One special feature, the *kanban* system, received particular attention. "Just-in-Time" (JIT), another Toyota concept, became fashionable and resulted in a proliferation of JIT engineers and JIT institutes.

The old-style managers who first created the Toyota Production System designed their plants based on traditional notions; their casting, forging, welding, painting, and assembly shops were all physically separated from one another. To link these shops, they needed to be able to transmit production instructions indicating what, how much, and when. Taiichi Ohno came up with the idea of controlling the number of instruction slips *(kanban)* in order to minimize stocks generated between processes. This approach had many advantages. As it became an independent system, many people throughout the world declared the Toyota Production System to be the same as a kanban system.

Had Taiichi Ohno contributed to the creation of Toyota's production system in the first place, the system would probably have been designed quite differently. Ohno no doubt created the kanban system as a "next best" approach in recognition of the serious drawbacks of moving machines and equipment already in place. Yet many managers and scholars think of this "next best" kanban system as the ideal. They imitate its visible, superficial techniques and promote it as the best system available. It seems to me that this attitude simply ends up impeding progress toward a better production system.

IS JIT A SHAM?

Given that some people who place special emphasis on the JIT system use the term only as a slogan, should we worry about how JIT is being interpreted from one place to the next? Some people even seem to suggest that JIT is a system of fixed techniques. Is this in fact the case?

There is no question that implementing a so-called JIT system may possibly raise productivity from 50 to 80 percent. What concerns me, however, is that the very practices that bring productivity to 80 percent might kill any possibility of raising it to 100 percent.

Studying a valid production system requires both (1) a "know-why" approach and (2) efforts toward attaining an even better system. I firmly believe, moreover, that one of the major objectives of a production system must be the relentless improvement of process functions.

TYPE-X AND TYPE-Y PEOPLE

We mentioned earlier that in 1960 Douglas McGregor of the Massachusetts Institute of Technology claimed that two opposing characteristics are found in human beings: Type X and Type Y. Both characteristics are present in each of us, and only their relative proportions differ. Briefly, Type X designates the desire to shirk work whenever possible and Type Y denotes an active willingness to work.

When Europe discovered the New World, many people were given new opportunities to work. As factories spread, a massive demand for labor drew multitudes of people from other parts of the world, such as Europe, South America, and Africa. However, while these people had all experienced work before, they were unaccustomed to a factory environment. Before, they used their labor to satisfy their own survival needs for food, clothing, and shelter. Offering their services — sometimes for work they disliked — in exchange for wages was a new concept.

By the 1880s, management was dissatisfied and concluded that workers were basically lazy. Workers, in their minds, were all Type-X people and nothing more than providers of labor. Management consequently felt free to fire workers when business was slow and hire workers when business picked up. The result was that the lives of workers became chaotic and wages remained low. In turn, workers joined together to form labor unions and use their collective might to stand up to management. Using force and strikes to return management's blows, adversarial labor unions arose.

A theory of class struggle emerged with its dreary view of society. These perceptions fomented unrest and created a climate favorable to the rise of socialism and communism. Much of the subsequent strife in the world would probably have given way to harmony had managers of the early 1880s defined workers as Type-Y instead of Type-X people.

At any rate, based on the assumption that the stimulus of wages would squeeze more work out of people, the managers of that era developed the piecework system of paying workers. Unfortunately, the vagueness of task and time standards needed to assign piece rates in a piecework system led to a repeated cycle in which workers felt they would be exploited regardless of how hard they worked. The cycle was as follows:

- Workers would increase their wages by working a little harder.
- Managers would conclude piece rates were too high and lower wages.
- Workers would make even greater efforts to increase their wages.
- Manager would once again lower piece rates.

The result was a kind of institutional sloth, or "soldiering." By mutual consent, union members refused to work very hard because hard work only resulted in lowered piece rates. And incentive pay, in the end, had no effect.

Around this time, Frederick Taylor was promoted from laborer to foreman and he wondered why soldiering occurred in the first place. He concluded that vague standards were the cause and decided that more scientific standards were needed to prevent output from being affected by unusually strenuous efforts.

Taylor's method was as follows:

Step 1. Analyze and break down work into small elemental tasks.

Step 2. Thoroughly study those elemental tasks and eliminate waste.

Step 3. Combine the remaining elemental tasks into a logical standard operation.

Step 4. Run piecework operations by setting a piece rate based on the time needed to perform this standard operation.

This "high efficiency, high wages, and low cost" approach streamlined production to a degree previously unimagined and did much to improve worker motivation.

Completely independently of Taylor, Frank and Lillian Gilbreth introduced the world to the concept of efficiency. Their idea was to make production thoroughly rational by the following steps:

Step 1. Analyze the facts in detail.

Step 2. Pursue work goals by asking the question *"why?"* at least three times.

Step 3. Bear in mind that there are several means to any one goal. (All progress would be impossible if every goal had only one means.)

Step 4. Identify the "one best way" to perform the task in the present circumstances.

At about the same time, I was wondering why there was such a surprising disparity in productivity between the Taiwan Government-General's Sungshan Railway Works and mainland Japanese railway plants. In the 1930s, I was so impressed by reading Taylor's *The Principles of Scientific Management* that I decided to enter the field of production "rationalization." Later, in 1937, Ken'ichi Horigome, managing director of the Japan Management Association, provided me with a thorough grounding in Gilbreth's philosophy during a two-month seminar in Tokyo. Ever since, production improvement has been my life's work.

Dr. Horigome had learned the philosophy of improvement from Engineering Lieutenant Jirō Kakuda of the Yokosuka Navy Yard. Kakuda had spent two months studying the concepts and techniques of improvement at Gilbreth's institute in the United States. Dr. Horigome was a fanatical believer in Gilbreth and demanded that we make at least one operational improvement every day during the two-month course. I, too, was profoundly impressed by Gilbreth. Indeed, the philosophies of Horigome and Gilbreth form the backbone of my own thinking.

While the view of workers just described permeated American industrial circles in the 1880s, at the time it never occurred to anyone to change Type-X into Type-Y characteristics. The temper of the times equated production with operations, and although the idea of a process component to production appealed to Gilbreth, he buried his own insight with the claim that processes lay on the same axis as operations.

In 1927, George Elton Mayo and his colleagues carried out the Hawthorne Works experiments in order to demonstrate the effect of lighting on work. As expected, output rose when illumination in the workplace was increased, but output also rose when the level of light was gradually lowered. The experimenters were unable to explain these results, but a psychologist's study showed that output was being sustained by the "mental tension" of workers who knew they were under scrutiny. This meant that, in contrast to previous improvements focusing merely on technical aspects of work, one also had to pay attention to psychological factors, or so-called human relations.

These experiments identified what McGregor called Type-Y characteristics. Rather than simply exploiting those characteristics in approaches such as Management by Objectives (MBO) and zero defect campaigns, however, it occurred to me to wonder why we could not take the approach of trying to change Type-X into Type-Y characteristics.

In 1968, Volvo president Pehr Gyllenhammar advocated abandoning conveyor systems in a book titled *People at Work: Surpassing the Ford System*. Gyllenhammar's argument repudiates the monotony of overly specialized tasks and the coercion of the conveyor line. In doing so, he accepts the notion that humans are basically Type-X creatures. Sweden is an extreme example of a welfare state. Public assistance is available not only to the needy — such as single mothers, the infirm, and the elderly; even healthy young people can live on unemployment benefits. Workers just out of school have 35 percent of their salaries taken in taxes, and a university professor I know claims his income is taxed at the rate of 85 percent. Seeking out Type-Y characteristics must be difficult in such an environment.

In Japan, on the other hand, the scarcity of natural resources makes individual labor crucial to personal happiness and national prosperity. Type-Y characteristics are considered a necessity in Japan, and a variety of institutions support these tendencies. These institutions offer lifetime employment, daily and monthly wage systems, relatively high wages, and profit sharing, although this last element has lost some of its significance recently.

Why are efforts to shift Type-X to Type-Y characteristics nearly inconceivable in the West? Why is it assumed that everyone is irretrievably, though regrettably, dominated by Type-X tendencies? Production activities in Europe and the United States cannot be expected to evolve unless attention and effort focus on this issue.

Granville-Phillips outside of Denver, Colorado, and Omark Industries in Portland, Oregon, have brought out Type-Y characteristics in their employees. In the process, they have achieved both high employee wages and high company profits.

We cannot hope for continued prosperity in the future until (1) we revise the old-style managerial perceptions of workers as lazy and (2) we return to the basic principle of enlarging the whole pie and dividing it more fairly among workers and management.

Finally, given that human nature and technology are quite different aspects of production, I cannot help but think that Volvo has seriously missed the point in claiming that its humanistic management has gone beyond the Ford system.

SHORTCOMINGS IN PRODUCTION MANAGEMENT AND CONTROL

In the West, following Dr. W. Edwards Deming's precepts, the functions of management are thought to consist of PLAN, DO, and CHECK (see Figure 7-1). The real functions of management, however, are PLAN, CONTROL, and CHECK — with DO occupying precisely the same space as CONTROL. The correct way to view the CONTROL function is as a function that constrains implementation, making it possible to DO according to plan. Figure 7-2 illustrates this principle.

The control function may be exercised by managers, or it may be thought of as the constraining function by which operators who know the standard operations check themselves.

U.S.-style quality control identifies a defect that results from some problem, feeds that information back, and then takes action.

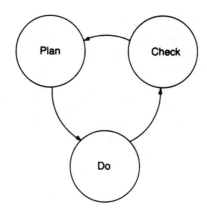

Figure 7-1. The Deming Circle

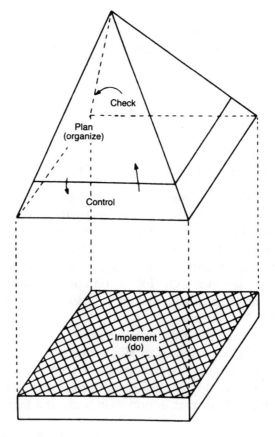

Figure 7-2. Management Cycle

Since the check performed is like a postmortem examination, however, it can never serve as an immediately effective improvement and cannot prevent the defect from occurring in the future.

On the other hand, immediate corrective action will prevent a defect from occurring in the first place if during the implementation (DO) process the control function addresses conditions that may cause the defect. This makes it possible to have a system in which source inspections completely eliminate defects.

In production, not generating defects is more important than finding defects. Not generating defects, however, requires a control function during the implementation process. Control is therefore a management function we cannot permit ourselves to overlook. The control function is necessary, not just for quality control, but for all facets of production management. In this sense, management functions as understood in the West contain a glaring omission.

DOES THE PRODUCTION CYCLE TURN WITH A SPIRAL MOTION?

We engage in production activities every day of the year — production activities that may be characterized as cycles of PLAN, CONTROL, and CHECK — with DO on the other side of CHECK. A rotation of this cycle can occur either in a plane or in an ascending spiral.

When the cycle is two-dimensional, consisting simply of an order, its production and delivery, the size of profits will be influenced by the diameter of the loop and the speed of the cycle. Yet, while there may be variations in the magnitude of profit in a two-dimensional loop, the size and speed of the cycle may have no effect at all on the profit rate. To increase the rate, we need qualitative improvements in production — or improved productivity.

The well-known phenomenon of rising revenues and decreasing profits comes about precisely because companies focus exclusively on increasing production volume and forget about improving production quality. It is not unusual for companies concentrating on quantitative expansion to be dazzled by big numbers and then go bankrupt when the books are balanced. We must always work to increase the *rate* of profits by pursuing qualitative improvements in production.

The difference between quantitative profit increases and increasing the profit rate tends to cause confusion. Therefore, it is essential to maintain a clear understanding of the distinction.

CIRCLE ACTIVITIES AND COMPANYWIDE CAMPAIGNS

U.S. quality control methods using inductive statistics first made their way to Japan in 1951. Rational techniques such as control charts and statistical sampling quickly spread throughout the nation. But the methods did not always penetrate to the workplace because front-line shop supervisors and operators needed to understand complex statistical procedures.

At this point, the Japanese used their propensity for group action to form QC circles to promote an interest in quality, to spur local efforts at quality improvement, and to help people understand the techniques of quality control. These efforts resulted in an unimagined heightening of quality awareness — and product quality soared.

Companies went on to expand the scope of their activities horizontally to all five management sectors and vertically to every level of their organizations. From top management on down, all employees participated in "Total Quality Control" (TQC) campaigns. A growing interest in quality control inevitably led to improved quality, and Japanese TQC campaigns began to be praised throughout the world.

What specific quality control philosophies were used in this movement? In the beginning, two kinds of inspections predominated:

- *Judgment inspection* does nothing but distinguish between acceptable and defective items. Quality control based on judgment inspections cannot reduce the rate of defects.
- *Informative inspection* is a method of quality control founded on a revolutionary and rational concept that makes it possible to reduce the defect rate. When a defect

occurs, a check is made and information is fed back to the source of the problem. On the basis of that information, action is then taken to prevent future defects.

Even informative inspections, however, have some serious deficiencies:

1. Because checks and feedback are carried out after the defect has occurred, informative inspections cannot reduce defects to zero.
2. Informative inspections require the use of control charts and sampling inspections based on the science of inductive statistics.

One wonders if perhaps quality control (QC) circle activities and companywide "total" campaigns were devised to compensate for these deficiencies. Thus, despite the fact that informative inspections and QC promotion campaigns serve quite different functions, they were publicized — erroneously, I believe — as being inseparable.

My view is that quality improvement in Japan is 85 percent attributable to QC circle activities and companywide campaigns and only 15 percent a result of the basic concept of informative inspections. We urgently need to create new quality control methods that overcome the fundamental shortcomings of informative inspections. My own response to this need is addressed in my book *Zero Quality Control: Source Inspection and the Poka-Yoke System* (Productivity Press, 1986).

Zero Quality Control (ZQC) makes it possible to eliminate defects entirely with simple techniques and at low cost. It goes without saying that QC circle activities and companywide campaigns will be needed to promote the use and spread of the ZQC system.

TQC, Total Productive Maintenance (TPM), and other promotional campaigns need to be thought of as distinct from management or control philosophies. The effectiveness of promotion campaigns and the inherent superiority of production management functions are different things. We need to be warned sternly against any illusions that might keep us from seeing them as clearly distinct (see Figure 7-3).

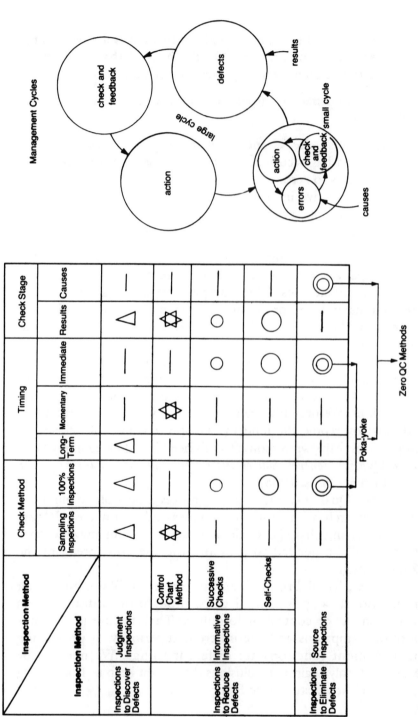

Figure 7-3. The Error/Control Cycle

THE FUNDAMENTALS OF IMPROVEMENT

If we look at improvement activities worldwide, the most original contribution was probably the development of the division of labor in England in the 1750s. Although Adam Smith writes about it, we are still uncertain who first came up with the idea.

In the next era, Frederick W. Taylor's procedure for establishing standard work for piecework systems was as follows:

- Analyze the work in detail.
- Study it exhaustively.
- Determine tasks scientifically.
- Establish solid standard times based on a little extra effort.

But what do "exhaustive study" and "scientific tasks" really mean? Taylor invented high-speed steel in 1898, but the conceptual process that led to its discovery is not clear.

Gilbreth finished his famous study of bricklaying, published *Motion Study* in 1912, and made "therbligs" public in 1912. He was the first to explain the conceptual process of improvement and referred to that process as the "motion mind":

1. Analyze the work in detail (using *therbligs*).
2. Pursue goals by asking the question *"why?"* at least three times.
3. Bear in mind that there are several means to any one goal.
4. Identify the "one best way."

Because this formulation is too simple, however, I have subdivided Gilbreth's conceptual stages and elaborated a process that deals with problems systematically and leads to the point where improvements actually materialize. I strongly urge the reader to never lose track of the steps of this Scientific Thinking Mechanism (STM). These steps summarize the STM I first presented publicly in 1957:

1. How do we identify problems?
2. Analyze the facts in greater detail.
3. Pursue goals (from X, Y, and Z perspectives).
4. Devise an improvement plan.
   - Observe.

- Formulate ideas. (This must not be done at the same time as observation.) Use associative thinking to generate ideas.
- Make judgments. (Do not judge at the same time as idea formulation. Use Osborne's brainstorming techniques.)
- Implement a plan using approaches presented in Dale Carnegie's books.
- Understanding is not sufficient. People will not take action unless they are convinced. Understanding is a cognitive function; being convinced is an emotive one.

In Europe and the United States I am frequently asked what prompts me to come up with ideas no one else has thought of before — ideas such as the single-minute exchange of die (SMED), source inspections and mistake-proof *poka-yoke* devices that totally eliminate defects, and non-stock production. I reply by saying that my teacher was Dr. Ken'ichi Horigome, former managing director of the Japan Management Association. Dr. Horigome's teacher was Engineering Lieutenant Jirō Kakuda of the Yokosuka Naval Yard — and his teacher was Frank B. Gilbreth.

At this point, I frequently ask why Gilbreth, an American, has been forgotten in his own country. Even today, I firmly believe that Gilbreth's "motion mind" approach, hammered into me by Dr. Horigome in Tokyo in 1937, forms the backbone of my own view of improvement.

In the final analysis, I believe the key to improvement lies in understanding and mastering a fundamentals-oriented improvement philosophy and the techniques to make improvement happen. Obviously, one also needs a correct understanding of the object of improvement — the structure and functions of production. I will discuss these issues, but for now I cannot overemphasize the absolute and fundamental importance of understanding and mastering the philosophy and techniques of improvement.

A critical review of current production systems allows an understanding of the basic flaws in conventional production management improvement to open up new directions for future progress.

8

Improvement Misunderstood

All improvements result in better situations than before. That doesn't mean, however, that all improvements are equal. Some improvements are only way stations to higher-level improvements. There are even some improvements in a specific production area that people flatter themselves into thinking will improve all production functions. These are all one-sided improvements.

In the final analysis, how we look at improvement objectives determines the kind of improvements we end up with.

FUNDAMENTAL VERSUS SUPERFICIAL

Lopsided improvements are indisputably improvements — but they are only superficial ones. We have to go deeper and make fundamental improvements.

Economic Lots and the SMED Concept

In Japan, as in the United States and Europe, scholars have explained at length the need for economic lots. As shown in Figure 8-1, their thinking is this:

- Individual product costs will decrease as the size of processing lots increases.
- Processing lots that are too large, however, generate stock (inventory) that entails costs.
- We must aim for an "economic" lot size defined by the point at which these two effects are balanced.

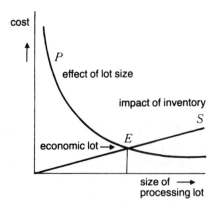

Figure 8-1. Economic Lot Size

This orthodox argument, however, overlooks a major point. The claim that costs decrease as lot sizes increase makes the assumption that setup changeover times are long. If a setup that used to take four hours were cut to three minutes, then the proportional impact of the changeover would be minimal. Today we can find setups being reduced to thirty seconds or less, further diminishing any effect of an economic lot size.

Rather than concentrate on the superficial question of economic lots, we should instead look at the real source of the problem — the drastic reduction of setup times.

Inventory Control and the Automated Warehouse

On a visit to a major U.S. company, I was told at the final process that all parts inventories are managed by computer. My guide told me his plant used a multistory automated warehouse that could retrieve any desired part within three minutes. Invited to choose a card for the system to read, I selected one at random and handed it to the operator. As soon as the card was inserted in the reader, the automated warehouse began working. It picked up a part from a high rack in the back and, indeed, brought it to us in two minutes and forty seconds. The engineering manager who was showing me the plant asked me if I was surprised.

"Indeed I am," I told him. "It's marvelous!"

"Do you have equipment like this in Japan," he asked.

"We certainly don't," I replied.

"I didn't think so!" he said proudly.

"I don't think you understand," I said. "In Japan we produce parts 'just in time.' In other words, we only make what the assembly process needs in the quantity and at the time it needs it. So, you see, we don't need parts warehouses like this."

My guide looked rather glum and said no more.

Which is the wiser approach: (1) investing millions of dollars in an automated warehouse or (2) using a system of production management that doesn't require a warehouse in the first place?

A Better Way to Deburr

In both Japan and the West, I am always asked how to remove burrs quickly. My stock answer is simple. I simply say, "Don't make burrs in the first place!" And people always reply, "But you can't avoid burrs!"

Burrs needn't be generated if you shear the material with blades coming from above and below, like a pair of scissors. Most cutting tools are pushed through the material they cut, however, and burrs are dragged out when the unopposed tool blade leaves the material. By placing a piece of scrap plate behind the piece to be cut, burrs will be generated on the scrap but not on the product.

When I'm in a plant, we run a test right away and the product always comes out burr-free. In one instance, San'ei Kinzoku KK in Kyūshū completely eliminated burrs by drilling through half of a 1.6-millimeter steel plate from above and then drilling the other half of the hole from below.

Plastic Vacuum Molding

On a trip to Daimler-Benz in Germany to teach the SMED system, I visited the plant's diecasting shop. When I found their products had no flash, I asked what they had done to eliminate it. I was told that the plant used low-pressure casting in which air was removed from the dies after the die blocks were clamped together. The molten material was then injected into the vacuum in the dies.

I realized at that point that die injecting operations consisted of exchanging molten material for air. I felt as though I understood for the first time the place of air on earth!

It seemed to me that the principle I had learned would work for both diecasting and plastic molding. Once back in Japan, I asked Yasuhide Tsukamoto, the president of Daiya Plastics in Osaka Prefecture, to make a vacuum die. In short order, the die was made and defects fell drastically with the following results:

- Bare spots, which occur when not enough material packs into one part of the product, vanished.
- Pinholes disappeared.
- Shot cycle times were shortened.

In the past, contact between the mobile die and the stationary die demanded very high precision. It was extremely difficult to expel air and at the same time prevent the escape of resin. Having a vacuum inside the die now meant that resin could be injected at low pressure. Flash, moreover, was completely eliminated.

In Toyota City, Tōgō Seisakusho under its president, Tōichi Aiba, was able to raise forming machine productivity by 65 percent by adopting vacuum forming for spring knobs. The cost of fitting dies with O-rings, providing a vacuum pump and hoses, and so forth is on the order of $8,000. When a 65 percent productivity increase is achieved on a plastic molding machine costing $52,000, however, the profit is substantial.

ULTIMATE IMPROVEMENTS AND INTERMEDIATE IMPROVEMENTS

We have already noted that sometimes people confuse intermediate or interim improvements with ultimate improvements.

They satisfy themselves with some intermediate step and neglect higher-level improvements.

The Toyota Production System and the Kanban System

When I mention the Toyota Production System in the United States and Europe, people's first reaction is often, "Oh, you mean the kanban system, right?"

As far as they are concerned, the Toyota Production System and the kanban system are the same thing! Their perception, in other words, is that the Toyota Production System does not exist apart from a kanban system. Even in Japan, there are scholars who, when discussing the Toyota Production System, proceed to talk only about kanban.

In contrast, my view is that one of the great failings of the Toyota Production System is its reliance on the kanban system. As I explained earlier, kanban are clumsy devices necessitated by the fact that casting and forging processes are not linked to machining and assembly processes. If processes were linked in the first place, there would be no need for kanban.

Certain scholars and managers have proposed the use of various types of kanban as an ideal. Such claims, however, only illustrate their ignorance about the basic functions of production.

Multiprocess handling is loudly touted as well, but multiprocess handling is needed only because bits of human tasks remain in the production process. By carrying out a higher level of pre-automation, the need for human multiprocess handling will vanish because human assistance will no longer be necessary.

The benefits of tasks at which operators can assist one another in multiprocess handling operations have been pointed out as well. Here, again, a more consequential approach would be to make exhaustive efforts to stabilize operations so that assistance would not be needed for tasks between processes. Neglecting efforts to stabilize operations in order to emphasize a strategy of "shared tasks" is a topsy-turvy way of viewing the problem.

At Matsushita Electric's Washing Machine Division, washer bodies emerging from the blanking press move directly to a conveyor that takes them to be painted and bent. There are no pauses in the overall operation and the finished product comes off the line in two and a half hours. Since there are no pauses during this period, kanban are not needed and stocks are at a bare minimum. Surely this arrangement is a more preferable and sophisticated production system than any kanban method.

COMPREHENSIVE IMPROVEMENTS VERSUS LOCAL IMPROVEMENTS

In contrast with maintenance activities that take place after machine abnormalities have occurred, preventive maintenance (PM) seeks to keep equipment problems from happening in the first place. Preventive maintenance deserves high marks in the sense that its methods resemble "well patient" checkups rather than postmortem examinations. In addition, the PM approach can bring about substantial improvement when linked to companywide activities in a Total Productive Maintenance (TPM) system. The relentless pursuit of machine functions called for by skills engineering, too, can lead to previously unimagined success.

Another dramatically successful technique is the "pack" system, which can raise productivity three or four times. The pack system combines the advantages of the relentless improvement of specific tasks and a heightened worker awareness of performance brought about by an American-style incentive pay system.

Each of these systems, however, focuses on the improvement of operations or tasks, and none can fairly be called a comprehensive approach for improving all production activities — including process functions. In this sense, local improvements may not be tied to improvements in overall production. Reducing defects or inventories to zero may, of course, have some partial effect, but they should not be confused with systems to make the entire production system more rational.

While some engineers endorse TPM as a panacea for improving production as a whole, I think the proper approach involves an understanding of the limitations of local remedies.

A CONFUSION OF MEANS AND GOALS

Eighteen spot welders at Koga Kinzoku Kōgyō KK weld 8.2 million automobile parts each month. For the last five years, the company has achieved zero defects by installing a "Zero" QC system I created. The system at Koga, which uses roughly 60 source inspection sensors linked to a system of mistake-proof *poka-yoke* devices to carry out immediate action and 100 percent inspections, required a monetary investment of approximately $8,000.

Koga at one point was visited by a Mr. N, the officer in charge of quality control at Koga's parent company. N reprimanded the Koga plant for failing to be more attentive to quality control. When asked what he was referring to, N declared that not a single control chart was on display and that a shop foreman had shown total incomprehension when asked about a simple QC term like "3S."

Yoshiaki Yamaura, the Koga manager who told me the story, asked me if he needed control charts even if there were no defects as demonstrated in Photo 8-1.

Photo 8-1. Koga Kinzuko photo commemorating the achievement of 8.2 million parts without a single welding defect.

"If you have to post control charts," I told him before leaving, "just draw a straight horizontal line for your mean value. And if they say you need to draw in control limits, just tell them Dr. Shingo said you didn't have to."

On my next visit to the company, I asked Yamaura what had become of the control chart episode. He replied that N had gone back and told his own manager about it and that he had gotten a chewing out. That was the last Yamaura had heard of the matter.

For N, the problem lay in implementing a *means* — control charts — while the real *goal* of eliminating defects was of no interest. Some people mistake means and goals and allow themselves to be distracted by the issue of implementing what is only a means. This phenomenon is surprisingly common in production plants.

FRONT AND SIDE VIEWS OF PRODUCTION FUNCTIONS

As we have already seen, production consists of a network of processes and operations and operations are subordinate to processes. We must therefore see processes as a "front view" of production and operations as a supplementary "side view."

The function of building engine cylinders of cast steel is actually accomplished by operations such as drilling and forming. We see such consummatory "operations" in an entirely different light, however, when a fixed *string of processes* produces welded structures via, say, the bending of metal plates, welding, and the grinding of seams. As noted above, devising a *process* that generates no burrs makes deburring *operations* totally unnecessary.

We may therefore view production first and foremost as consisting of front-view process activities whose functions are actually accomplished by side-view operations. Processes always precede operations, but are often overlooked because operations weigh more heavily in the actual accomplishment of production functions. Anyone who gives the matter serious thought can understand that operational functions must never precede process functions. See Figures 8-2 and 8-3 for visual interpretations of these ideas.

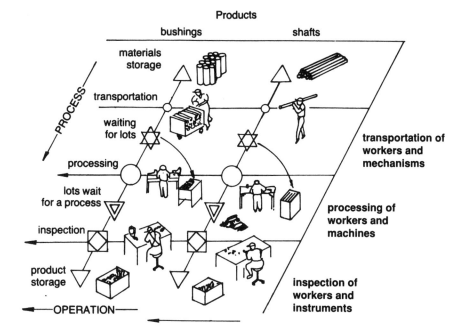

Figure 8-2. Processes and Operations

SLOGANS AND SUBSTANCE

In 1988 I delivered an address in Toronto sponsored by the Canadian Automobile Parts Association, an organization through which Toyota, Nissan, and Honda provide education and consulting services to Canadian auto parts manufacturers.

In discussions preceding my talk, I was told that the "Big Three" U.S. auto makers — General Motors, Ford, and Chrysler — had heard of the Toyota Production System in which Toyota needs to order only what it wants, when it wants it, and in the quantities it wants. This sounded like a convenient approach to the "Big Three" and, without any prior notification, they suddenly began demanding JIT deliveries: "Part A by 10:00 tomorrow morning" and "Part B by 2:00 tomorrow afternoon." Their suppliers were thrown into utter confusion, deadlines were missed, parts ran out, and production schedules fell apart. For their part, the suppliers never knew when orders would come in, and soon they were choked by rising inventories.

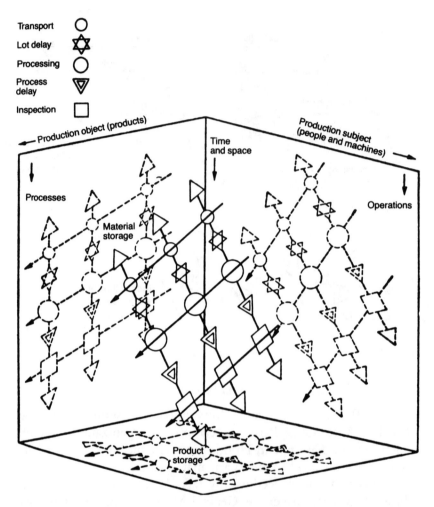

Figure 8-3. Three-dimensional Structure of Production

In my talk I responded that it had taken Toyota Motors ten years to perfect the Just-in-Time system in-house. During those ten years, Toyota used the SMED system to increase production schedule elasticity and worked to minimize production lead times by using small lots and the one-piece flow system. Once the system was up and running within Toyota itself, the company loaned its production engineers and managers to the plants of its principal suppliers, where they gave counsel and ran experiments until nearly all the suppliers understood — and were persuaded by — the system. It was another ten years before this work among suppliers bore fruit. Therefore, it actually took Toyota twenty years to put in place a full-scale JIT system. Toyota's suppliers reaped huge benefits from the system, and all companies affiliated with the auto maker worked to develop and expand the new system.

I told my audience that the smooth implementation of the new system by Toyota and its suppliers took place only after massive preparations. The system could never have succeeded if the parent company had tried to impose it unilaterally and arbitrarily. "Look what happened at Company R in France," I said, "where the experiment failed after three months because suppliers revolted and refused to make deliveries!"

This brought a great roar of applause from the audience, and later I heard that the system of demands for immediate deliveries collapsed not long afterward.

As this story illustrates, failure inevitably comes of swallowing slogans and making unilateral proposals for "rationalization." Unfortunately, many shortsighted managers think slogans are the answer. So-called JIT institutes and JIT managers have proliferated in recent years. It is sobering to wonder how many of them really understand Just-in-Time.

THE SAFETY MOVEMENT IN JAPAN

I once happened to visit Volkswagen in Germany when mechanical failure had shut down a 300-ton press. A technician opened the door of the protective cage, went inside, and fixed the problem. He then pushed an ON button inside the enclosure but the machine did not start until he had opened and closed the door again. This two-stage switch system impressed me: workers were protected because activating the switch inside the enclosure was not enough to start the machine.

Let's compare this approach to the safety movement in Japan, campaigns consisting merely of slogans intended to raise awareness of safety. The Japanese safety movement consists entirely of slogans and does nothing more than make a lot of noise during the "Safety Month" of July. The probability is very high that the person who submits the prize-winning slogan one day will have an accident the following day.

Daimler-Benz does not allow presses to be used unless they have been provided with safety devices. Users of presses adhere to the following set procedures:

- Place the part on a feeder outside the press.
- When the front shield opens, insert the feeder in the die inside the press and place the workpiece.
- The feeder returns and the shield closes.
- The press ram descends.
- The workpiece is then removed from the press by reversing the same movement.
- It is impossible to insert hands into the press while the machine is operating.

This approach results in much lower accident rates than in Japanese companies. Accidents that do occur at Daimler-Benz are on the order of scrapes from slipping and falling on roads on the plant grounds.

Why does the Japanese safety movement go no further than calling for heightened awareness via slogans such as: "Attention costs a second; an accident costs a lifetime"? I have seen many factories abroad, but I have never seen plants so plastered with slogans and posters as are those in Japan.

Make no mistake here. I'm not saying that workers don't need to pay attention to their jobs. I am, however, arguing that safety shouldn't rely solely on "awareness." We need to change our orientation as soon as possible to one in which paying attention and being careful complement a basic reliance on physical devices to assure safety.

ESSENTIAL IMPROVEMENTS AND SUPPLEMENTARY IMPROVEMENTS

As we have already seen, informative inspections backed by sophisticated inductive statistics are essential to quality control in the QC movement. The QC approach breaks with traditional methods by using statistically-based sampling inspections and control charts to categorize abnormal values. It is from these techniques that statistical quality control derives its authority. Promoted on a broad scale through QC circles and "Total" QC campaigns, statistical quality control has enjoyed enormous popularity. The "total employee involvement" (TEI) aspect of the movement, however, is like seasoning on food: it doesn't necessarily reflect the underlying flavor of the meal.

No approach founded on informative inspections can ever eliminate all defects because checks, feedback, and action are carried out only *after* defects have been generated. Since every defect is the result of some underlying error or malfunction, source inspections and mistake-proof *poka-yoke* devices can lead to zero defects when combined with prompt action to suppress abnormalities at the error stage. Source inspections check for errors, and inexpensive, easy-to-use *poka-yoke* devices allow for 100 percent inspections instead of sampling inspections. Significant results can be obtained by linking source inspections and *poka-yoke* devices with TEI campaigns.

Total employee involvement is such a delicious seasoning that it can have a favorable impact on preventive maintenance in the form of TPM. It can also be used for safety campaigns and, indeed, would be immensely effective in a total non-stock system. However great its rewards may be, total employee involvement still remains a seasoning. We must not allow its benefits to distract us from basic flaws in production management functions.

A growing number of factories in Japan and the United States are shifting from statistical quality control to systems of source inspections and *poka-yoke* devices precisely because the "Zero" Quality Control (ZQC) system can eliminate defects altogether. Perhaps this trend reflects an understanding of the fact that TEI campaigns play a supplementary role — one that is distinct from the basic functions of production management.

KNOW-HOW AND KNOW-WHY

I will never forget something once told me by Akira Shibata, the former chairman of Taihō Kōyō. Shibata observed that the success of new, more rational methods brought in from one company to another may often be quite satisfactory. However, techniques acquired only as superficial "know-how" can be applied only to identical or similar tasks in the receiving plant. Such techniques are generally not applicable to different industries or unrelated tasks.

Shibata emphasized that the situation changes when, in spite of superficial differences, there is a sound understanding of the basic significance of the improvements — in other words, where there is "know-why." In this case, applying basic concepts can lead to improvement even in apparently unrelated work.

In one instance, Mr. Ohmizo, the manager of a woodworking plant, had been frustrated in his repeated attempts to visit another plant in the same industry. I suggested the problem was that he had been clinging too tightly to the idea of picking up know-how he could easily copy and use in his own plant. All he needed to do, I told him, was visit plants in different industries and learn know-why. He later reported that a visit to a metalworking plant had been extremely helpful because he had picked up a surprising number of ideas that had resulted in improvements unique to his industry. It was all possible because Ohmizo paid attention to grasping know-why.

Production appears in a myriad of forms, but focusing on methods rather than products narrows down superficial diversity to a limited number of component operations. This approach reveals a high degree of similarity and opens up numerous possible applications for improvement ideas. The lesson here is that, in considering improvements, we must always ascend beyond know-how to the higher vantage point afforded by know-why.

EXPANDING SUGGESTION PROGRAMS

One hears that Japanese-style suggestion *(teian)* systems have gained popularity in the United States recently — so much so that the Japanese word for improvement *(kaizen)* is even used to name some of them. Since it was the Ford Motor Company's suggestion system that provided the original idea for Japanese *teian* programs, it seems a little ironic that Japanese suggestion systems are now being re-imported into the United States. At any rate, I am concerned that lively Japanese suggestion systems might seem to certain enthusiasts to be in the business merely of collecting fortuitous suggestions.

It was Frank W. Gilbreth in the 1890s who first promoted the notion of scientific improvement thinking. In 1957 I amplified his basic ideas in my Scientific Thinking Mechanism (STM), a process systematically linking the identification of improvement possibilities, a grasp of the status quo, observation, idea formulation, judgment, proposed improvement, and implementation.

(For further reading, see *The Sayings of Shigeo Shingo: Key Strategies for Plant Improvement* [Productivity Press, 1987].)

While improvements may come in any number of guises, many improvements are misdirected. We need to re-examine the purposes and goals we are addressing.

9

Take Another Look
at Machine Functions

> Too often we fail to question the function of existing machinery.

CUTTING AIR WITH A PLANER

Planers, shapers, and other reciprocating cutting machines often do nothing but "cut air" on return strokes. Some people may protest that the return strokes are necessary for tools to return to home positions and that the time involved is insignificant.

I wondered at one point why machines couldn't cut on the return stroke as well, so I asked Tadanori Koga, the head of engineering at Koga Kinzoku, to modify a machine and allow the cutting tool to reverse at the end of the outbound stroke and cut on the return stroke. This innovation resulted in an 80 percent increase in productivity.

RESHAPING SPOT-WELDER TIPS

The following example comes from Glory Industries (Kanji Matsushita, chairman) in the city of Himeji.

The problem was to increase the life of spot welder tips that had to be reshaped every 300 welds. Going out on the shop floor to observe the operation, I saw the welder slam into a length of sheet metal. "Why does the welder tip have to strike so hard if all it has to do is pass current through the workpiece," I asked.

"That's to make sure the two sheets to be welded are in positive contact with one another," I was told.

We reduced wear on the tip by building a hydraulic clamping fixture to hold down the workpiece 1.5 millimeters from the tip. At this point, someone complained that the high resistance temperature necessarily softened the copper welding tip.

"Then cool the tip with low-temperature compressed air."

"But residue buildup on the tip will insulate it."

"In that case, clean the tip at the top of the stroke after each weld," I said. "In other words, don't clean tips when they get dirty. Clean them so that they never get dirty in the first place."

In the past, tips had to be reshaped every 300 welds. Simple devices to implement the above changes, however, resulted in tips that could still be used after more than 10,000 welds.

UNCONSTRAINED PRESS OPERATION

Most presses come to a full stop at the upper dead point. For safety reasons, they don't begin moving again until a check has been made to assure that the workpiece is fully held in the die. At Central Automobile KK (Sentoraru Jidōsha KK/Shōzō Akiyama, president), the position of the workpiece in the die is checked by sensors 30 degrees before the upper dead point is reached. Under ordinary circumstances, the press cycles continuously and stops only when some abnormality is detected. The result of this arrangement has been a 30 percent increase in the machine's operating rate and a significant reduction in wear on rotating parts. This considerable gain in productivity was achieved fairly smoothly despite strong initial shop-floor resistance on the grounds that the approach would damage the machine.

A DRILLING OPERATION
IMPROVEMENT: MORE EFFICIENT
CUTTING OIL AND A CHIP BREAKER

The disposal of chips poses a vexing problem in deep drilling operations. A certain Plant K took the following approach:

- Drill bits are designed with the ability to break off chips into small pieces that are easily carried away by cutting oil fed under pressure. (The point is that only the tips of the bits actually perform the cutting.)
- A small copper tube wound along one of two channels in the bit feeds cutting oil at high pressure to drive chips out the other channel. Effectiveness is further increased by spraying cutting oil through a hole bored in the core of the bit. These measures have yielded a 15 percent rise in drilling operation efficiency.

While cutting oil is generally thought of as providing a lubricating effect, it actually does three things in roughly the following proportions:

1. cools cutting edges   50 percent
2. carries away chips   40 percent
3. lubricates   10 percent

Cutting oil is especially effective in reducing wear by disposing of chips. The idea here is exactly the same as for gang drilling.

Part III

Improving Production
Management

10

The Object of Improvement

We must understand that production management improvement consists of two things:

The Improvement Mind-set	→	The Structure and Functions of Production

In Part I of this book, we presented problems and approaches to improvement. In Part II, we discussed basic improvement thinking. Since discussions in the past have often been conducted in the absence of a proper understanding of comprehensive, fundamentals-oriented production management improvement, in Part III we will focus on the object of improvement (that is, the structure and functions of production).

EXPLOITING DEMAND AND VALUE ENGINEERING

Exploiting demand is the first step in production management. This means two things:

1. clarifying and exploiting potential market needs, such as new product development

2. altering or modifying needs for existing products by such actions as adding new functions or reducing prices

Both of these issues need to be studied thoroughly from the perspective of value engineering and value analysis.

MANAGEMENT FUNCTIONS

This book has limited itself to questions involving production. Let us examine some other aspects of management. Executive management may be said to consist of five functional areas, as illustrated in Figure 10-1:

1. *Technical skills.* Obviously, production cannot take place without the basic and specific technical abilities needed to make the desired product (for example, thin stainless steel plate welding technology or composite casting technology).
2. *Finance.* After technical requisites, capital is needed to pay for such things as plant facilities and equipment, materials, and worker wages.

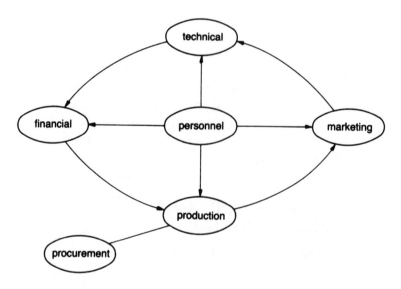

Figure 10-1. Five Functional Aspects of Management

3. *Production.* Production comprises the activities by which products are actually manufactured.
4. *Marketing.* A return on capital comes only when products are sold. At that point, the technical skill/finance/production/marketing cycle begins again.
5. *Personnel.* Management is carried out by people. Once an organization of people is built, a personnel department is needed to manage personnel-related aspects of the other four functional areas.

Although we will discuss only the role of production here, readers should note the relevance of many of these issues to other areas of management. We should also mention the need for an administrative function to handle communication among the other five functions.

THE PYRAMIDAL STRUCTURE OF MANAGEMENT

Although all production activities require managerial functions like those described below, the *control* function is absent in many companies. As shown in Figure 10-2, managing consists of the following stages:

1. *Wanting* → having the desire to make something
2. *Deciding* → resolving to go ahead and make it
3. *Planning* → laying out a program for making it
4. *Implementing* → actually making it
5. *Controlling* → ensuring that implementation proceeds as planned
6. *Monitoring* → checking the result of controlled implementation by comparison with the plan (Responses to any planning, implementation, or control problems identified are reflected in the next plan.)
7. *Satisfaction* → judging that the result of monitoring is, say, 100 percent or 80 percent acceptable, determining the next policy (such as wanting and deciding), and beginning the next cycle

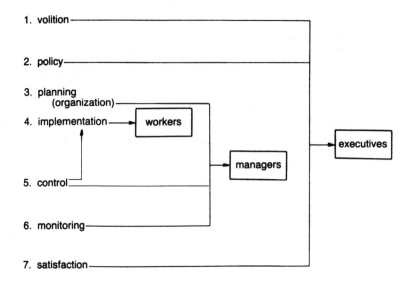

Figure 10-2. Seven Action Stages

The Deming PLAN-DO-CHECK cycle advocated in Europe and the United States lacks the control function and as a result tends to fulfill only extremely weak functions.

As we shall see later on, there is a major difference between the notions of informative inspections and "Zero" Quality Control (ZQC). The inability of informative inspections to reduce defects to zero marks a crucial distinction between such inspections and a system of source inspections and mistake-proof *poka-yoke* devices. Faithful adherence to ZQC can reliably reduce defects to zero.

CAD/CAM AND DESIGN

The use of computers, as in computer-aided design (CAD) and computer-aided manufacturing (CAM) techniques, can be very effective at the stage of generating designs for products and product components.

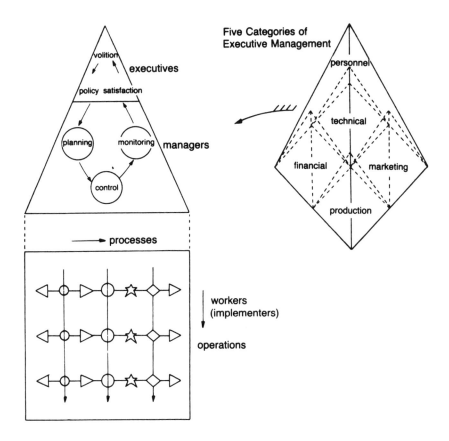

Figure 10-3. The Pyramidal Structure of Management

COMPUTERS AND INFORMATION MANAGEMENT

Information management is the means by which management is carried out. Computers make it possible to carry out numerous and effective management activities because:

- Computers rapidly accept massive amounts of information as input.

- Computers calculate and manipulate large quantities of information.
- Computers provide large amounts of information as output at once.

At the same time, people must carefully choose to input only information deemed important. Nonessential information must be avoided. Remember that a computer is not an end in itself. It is ultimately a tool that we must use wisely. Administrative work is mediated by time and space, moreover, and improvement in these areas can limit the use of computers to only truly essential functions.

In short, don't make the mistake of allowing yourself to be seduced by a tool just because the tool is a particularly handy one.

Part IV

The First Function of
Production Management:
Process Improvement

11

Process Functions

A *process* is a flow by which raw materials are transformed into finished products. Processes play the primary function in production — what we have called the "frontal view" function. Next are *operations*, functions we need to regard as secondary and complementary to process functions.

Process functions can be expressed by four different phenomena:

1. processing
2. inspection
3. transportation
4. delays

Processing involves changes in form and quality and in assembly and disassembly. Inspection involves comparisons with standards to avoid making defects. Transportation involves changes in location.

There are two types of delays: process delays and lot delays. Process delays are delays in which an entire processing lot waits for the previous lot to be completely processed. Synchronization can eliminate process delays. For the sake of convenience, the term "process delay" may include any waiting generated by lagging operations (such as running behind schedule, machine breakdowns, or rework).

Lot delays involve, for instance, a lot of 1,000 pieces in which 999 unprocessed pieces wait while the first piece is being processed.

While the second piece is being processed, 998 pieces wait in the unprocessed state. Similarly, the first piece to have been processed is delayed until the entire lot has been processed in order to synchronize movement of the lot. These delays can be eliminated by using "one-piece flow" operations between processes.

In a 1921 article in the journal of the American Society of Mechanical Engineers, Frank B. Gilbreth clearly stated that production is composed partly of processes and that processes consist of processing, inspection, transportation, and delays.

IMPROVING PROCESSING

Processing refers to acts that alter the form or quality and that assemble or disassemble.

- *Altering form* means changing the shape of an object by means of, for example, casting, forging, or machining.
- *Altering quality* means changing the state, quality, or composition of an object by heat treatment, tempering, or other means.
- *Assembling* means joining two parts into a whole either by fitting them together or by means of welding or similar processes.
- *Disassembling* means dividing a single item into two parts.

An issue that frequently arises is that processing acts that are process elements cannot be distinguished from operations.

Marking Off a Die Center

This example involves the task of centering dies used on a large press. Centering was necessary because off-center dies generated defective products. The conventional procedure had been to place the material on a surface plate and mark it off using a height gauge. Gauge instability due to excessive height had led to experimentation with a magnetic stabilization device. The considerable height and weight of the magnet, however, made positioning difficult for the operator who had to work on a stand.

In response to the problem, I suggested cutting a shallow center line in the wooden casting mold. Aligning the resulting line in the casting with the planer's center groove eliminated the need for a marking-off operation.

This is a perfect example of a process improvement as opposed to an operational improvement.

Polishing a Bed

One workshop used five grinding machines to polish beds. Therefore, because the machines had to be run overtime and on weekends to compensate for insufficient capacity, the shop asked for another grinder.

I decided to go out to the floor to view the process in question. There I saw a grindstone feed down onto a workpiece eleven times. At that point I asked the shop supervisor what work the machine was supposed to be doing. When he told me it was a polishing operation, I observed that the point of polishing was to impart a smooth, mirror-like surface to the product.

"Surely," I said, "that doesn't require eleven passes of a grindstone!"

The supervisor replied that current methods involved heat-treating the product surface and that the heat treatment induced distortions that needed to be corrected. "We're doing that with grinding wheels," he told me, "because the surface is too hard for an ordinary cutting tool to cut. In other words, we're grinding it."

"How much material do you need to take off to polish the surface," I asked.

"0.6 millimeter."

"And how much do you have to take off to both polish and correct the heat treatment distortion?"

"Probably about 0.9 millimeter," he said.

I had the plant buy a high-precision digital gauge for the milling machine at the previous process so that precisely 0.9 millimeter of the surface would be left to grind. The next time I had an opportunity to visit the plant, I was told they were processing what they needed with only three machines and no overtime. Here again we see an example of a process improvement.

Inspecting Screws

This problem involved the machining of precision adjustment screws for optical microscopes. Screws were taken off the lathe between intermediate and final machining operations, and a three-pin gauge was used to measure the effective diameter in order to determine how much material remained to be taken off.

I questioned why the operation was necessary at all. With a precision of 0.005 millimeter, weren't defect-generating errors introduced simply by the act of removing and remounting screws on the lathe in order to measure them? Yes, I was told, that was a problem.

"Look," I said, "you're thinking that you can't use a three-point gauge on the lathe, but all you need to measure is the effective diameter. Instead of insisting on measuring the diameter directly, why not use a dial gauge equipped with a pin beveled to match the pitch of the threads? That would allow you to measure the radius, which you would simply double to get the diameter."

In the improved operation, a limit switch controls cuts to 0.03 millimeter. The special gauge then is used to stop cutting once the allowable dimensions are achieved. This eliminates both the intermediate measuring operation and reduces defects to zero. Another instance of process improvement, this modification consolidated what had previously been two separate operations — machining and measuring.

Piping in a Tanker

Many pipes need to be connected in a tanker. Modern tankers are built in "blocks" in a construction system pioneered by Captain Yomogidani of the Kure Navy Yard. In this method, the hull of a ship is divided into 400 blocks of 30 to 50 tons, which are assembled in covered sheds. Only the final block-to-block assembly is performed out of doors, so that rain no longer halts operations. Parallel construction of the blocks has also meant a massive reduction in the production cycle. From 1955 to 1965, for example, building a 650,000-ton class tanker took ten months in England, seven months in Germany, and only four months in

Japan. I shortened that time to two months, thereby setting a world record.

The dangerous and inefficient work of installing engine room piping was a major bottleneck at the time I was working with tanker construction. Workers would stand on 80-centimeter planks in the dark engine room and install pipes at 1.5-meter intervals on all sides. When one level was completed, the workers would go down a steel ladder in one corner of the room and hang pipes at the next level. We decided to improve this operation as follows:

1. Pipes are installed while blocks are being assembled in the construction sheds.
2. Blocks are then assembled in the yard.
3. Pipe connections are realigned as necessary after block assembly is complete.

This method eliminated the danger of the operations and increased pipe installation efficiency fivefold. Some people had been concerned that pipes would be misaligned, but in actual practice, no fatal defects occurred even though some joints had to be corrected. This example shows the considerable advantage gained by reversing a process sequence.

Automobile Door Assembly

In my visits to major automobile assembly plants throughout the world, I have observed that doors are often mounted near the beginning of the final assembly line before interior trim and fittings are installed. This results in many wasted operations as workers constantly open and close doors to move parts into, and to work on, automobile interiors. It also causes wasteful transportation movement between parts racks and the line, because the racks have to be far enough away to accommodate the opening and closing of doors.

The current assumption is that doors must be installed at the start of final assembly. But why can't the finished doors be hung at the end of the assembly process? Or, at the very least, why not remove the doors at the beginning of final assembly and put them back on at the end of the line? Such a move would cut space in half around the line and significantly reduce wasted movement and transportation now performed by assembly workers.

Going one step further, such an arrangement would probably make it possible to supply parts to needed processes automatically. Rather than having assemblers carry parts to the line, parts would be automatically fed to the cars. The idea is that parts at the line would be actively delivered to assemblers instead of having them wait passively for assemblers to pick them up and transport them. In other words, transporting parts should not be part of assembly operations. This approach is now being taken on part of the assembly line at Central Motors. At Fiat in Italy and Mazda in Japan, automobile doors are removed at the head of the assembly line and reinstalled at the end of the line. These companies report some difficulty in keeping an even gap between the body and doors, and I have made some suggestions for resolving the problem. Here again, we see an example of process-oriented processing improvements.

Other Process-oriented Processing Improvements

The term "process-oriented processing improvements" can be applied to all improvements in which, for example, precision forging can do away with the need for machining, or modifications in machining methods can make subsequent deburring operations unnecessary.

Although we may always think of process improvements in connection with processing or machining, such improvements are often too little examined or simply passed over. This is unfortunate, because being able to find process-oriented processing improvements gives us a chance at scoring a two- or three-base hit, or maybe a home run. Ordinary operational improvements, by contrast, typically yield only single-base hits. This is why we need to pay extra attention to process-oriented processing improvements.

IMPROVING INSPECTION FUNCTIONS

The ostensible function of inspections is comparison with a standard, and their purpose is to prevent defects from occurring. We can distinguish three levels of inspections: judgment inspections, informative inspections, and systems of inspections at the source. See Figure 11-1 for an illustrated breakdown of these levels.

Judgment Inspections

These are inspections to distinguish between acceptable and defective products. Their effect is merely to reduce the number of defective items shipped to customers. Defect rates within the plant are not addressed.

Informative Inspections

When a defect occurs, that information is checked and fed back to the process where the defect was generated. Corrective action then improves the situation for the future, and the defect rate gradually falls.

Statistically based sampling inspections are used to reduce the effort of performing informative inspections. Abnormalities are defined according to 3 σ limit control charts and other techniques. Such approaches that apply theories of inductive statistics are reputed to be extremely scientific.

Systems of Source Inspections and Mistake-proof *Poka-yoke* Devices: Immediate Action Systems

The ZQC approach may be summarized as follows:

1. Defects are results — not causes. Therefore, checking once defects have occurred can never eliminate defects entirely.

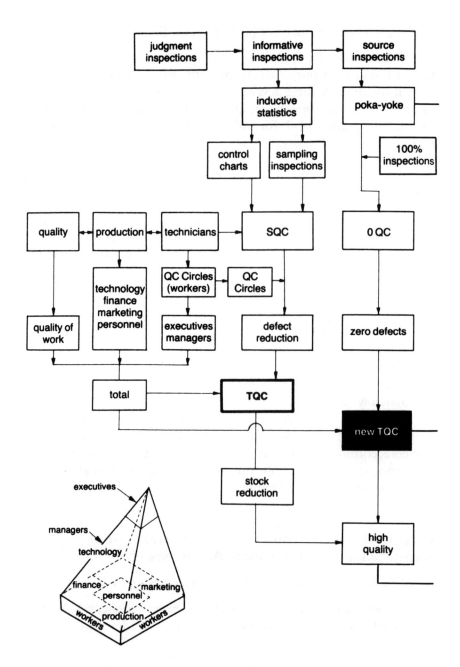

Figure 11-1. The New TQC

Checking at the stage of defect-causing errors and then carrying out feedback and action prevents errors from turning into defects in the first place.

2. Instead of sampling inspections, conduct 100 percent inspections incorporated into processing using mistake-proof *poka-yoke* devices that actively shut down machines and summon people when abnormalities occur. Whereas, people have to take the initiative in statistical QC, in a *poka-yoke* system sensors actively summon people — so everyone can relax. Also, the devices are inexpensive and function continuously once installed.

3. Corrective action is never delayed or forgotten because errors trigger immediate action in a control cycle that operates automatically. The occurrence of errors may cause temporal losses, but the system makes it possible to achieve absolutely no defects.

4. The regulatory functions of mistake-proof *poka-yoke* devices divide them into two categories: (1) "control types" that suppress the functions they govern and (2) "warning types" that use light or sound (such as buzzers or flashing lamps) to summon attention.

   Mistake-proof devices may be broken down further according to specific setting functions: (3) "contact types" that check dimensional differences based on whether or not contact is made, (4) "fixed value types" that check for deviations from predetermined values, and (5) "motion-step types" that check for errors in motions and sequences.

For an in-depth study, please see my book *Zero Quality Control: Source Inspection and the Poka-Yoke System* (Productivity Press, 1986).

IMPROVING TRANSPORTATION

In 1955, I had a conversation with Mr. Gozlan, the very able director of engineering at the F Company in France. Having observed that machines in his plant were laid out homogeneously, with similar machines clustered together, I asked him whether the resulting transportation wasn't inefficient. He replied that there was really no problem because chain conveyors carried items between the machines.

"Listen," I said, "chain conveyors may represent an improvement in transportation operations, but they don't improve transportation itself. You can come up with any kind of transportation means you want to, but it will never change the fact that transportation adds cost and not value.

Mr. Gozlan looked puzzled, but in March of the following year while in Japan on a study mission, he suddenly approached me and exclaimed that he understood what I had meant. He told me that French universities teach only homogeneous layouts and don't teach that transportation is waste. They assume that you can't make things without transportation and that transportation is an unavoidable but necessary evil.

Machine Layouts

We can classify machine layouts into four types:

1. process sequence-based layout
   a. single process sequence layout
   b. shared process sequence layout
   c. similar process sequence layout
2. product-based layout
   a. layout by families of similar parts
   b. layout by families of clustered parts
3. means-based layout
   a. homogeneous arrangement
4. irregular layout
   a. haphazard, unprincipled layout; layout in which machines are placed wherever there is a space for them

These layouts can be defined as follows:

- *Irregular layout* can be excluded from our discussion as it has no rhyme or reason.
- *Homogeneous layout* is an arrangement in which machines of a given type are placed together. Large and small ma-

chines are each grouped together even though they may be exactly the same type of equipment.

- *Product-based layouts* fall into two types:
  1. layout by part (such as cylinder-related machines, transmission-related machines, and carburetor-related machines)
  2. layout by families of similar parts (such as shaft-like products or plate-like products)
- *Process sequence-based layouts* comprise three types:
  1. single process sequence layout — a layout according to the process sequence for a single product
  2. shared process sequence layout — a layout grouping processes common to multiple products
  3. similar process sequence layout — a layout grouping processes with similar processes

Transportation Is a Sin

Grouping identical machine types in homogeneous layouts is extremely common. However, they generate significant transportation and are inefficient. "Transportation" is a phenomenon that always adds costs and not product value.

The prosperity of a resource-poor country like Japan rests solely on the high quality of its labor. Therefore, wasting labor on non-value-added work like transportation must be rejected. In fact, transportation should be seen as a grievous sin. Rather then try to make transportation operations more rational by bringing in apparatus such as forklifts and conveyors, we need to eliminate transportation altogether by improving layouts so that transportation is unnecessary in the first place. We must pay constant attention to this issue, because improvements in transportation operations and improvements in transportation itself are often confused.

In the beginning, machine layout methods were not based on any basic principles. In fact, no one understood why production activities gave rise to a need for transportation. The division of labor was an extremely effective tool, and people had no choice but to accept the transportation it invariably generated.

At some point, people thinking about operations must have come up with the homogeneous layout idea after deciding that the workplace would look neater if similar machines were lined up next to one another. They must have figured that grouping machines of the same type would facilitate the exploitation of capacity and make it easier for supervisors to manage equipment.

But if you look back at the essential nature of production activities, you gradually become aware that transportation never adds value in production. Let me re-emphasize that we must change our perception of transportation. We need to realize that, especially for a country as nearly devoid of natural resources as Japan, it is sinful to use our only precious resource — human beings — for the non-value-adding work of transportation. Unfortunately, the problem is generally thought of in terms of improving transportation operations rather than eliminating transportation itself, and efforts have concentrated on using cranes, forklifts, conveyors, and other forms of conveyance. In general, we have yet to realize that we should be eliminating transportation itself rather than improving forms of transportation.

Eliminating Twenty-two Forklifts

Various sophisticated techniques have recently led to significant gains at companies like those affiliated with Kanzaki Kōkyū Kōki KK, a manufacturer of machining center-equipped machine tools. They eliminated the need for twenty-two forklifts by combining shared and similar process sequence layouts with a one-piece flow system.

Once again, it is crucial to understand clearly that improving transportation itself and improving transportation operations are two different matters.

ELIMINATING DELAYS

The American production handbook differentiates between two types of delays or storage:

1. *Controlled storage* is storage provided for by a production plan.
2. *Temporary storage* is irregular storage that arises sporadically due to machine failures, missed delivery deadlines, and the like.

The sense of these terms was rendered in Japan as "process delays" *(kōteimachi)* and "temporary delays" *(ichijimachi)*, respectively. Until 1955, the distinction between the two was thought to be one of duration: Process delays were understood to be long-term delays, while temporary delays were seen as shorter. There was some confusion as to the cutoff point between them, and the vague figure of around thirty minutes came to be tacitly accepted.

The Discovery of Lot Delays

Investigations into the true nature of production activities, however, led to the discovery of another, qualitatively different kind of delay, called a "lot delay." Suppose we are processing a batch (or lot) of 1,000 pieces. While the first of these pieces is being processed, the other 999 pieces wait in the unprocessed state, and while the second piece is being processed, 998 pieces wait in the unprocessed state and one piece waits in the processed state. These periods of waiting are called lot delays, a phenomenon that Western schools of production management seemingly failed to acknowledge.

The most effective way to do away with lot delays is to adopt one-piece flow operations, in which each piece moves to the next process as soon as it has been processed. The only wrinkle is that, whereas processing in a 1,000-piece lot calls for only one transportation run after the entire lot has been processed, one-piece flow requires 1,000 transportation runs of one piece each. This creates a need for a process sequence-based layout and simple transport devices to move pieces easily from one process to the next. Using a one-piece flow system makes it possible to cut production lead times dramatically.

Delivery Cycles and Production Cycles

While we often complain about short delivery deadlines, we really need to look at the problem in terms of the relationship between the delivery cycle and the production cycle. A rush job may be inevitable if the delivery cycle (D) between order and delivery is one week and the production cycle (P) is two weeks. How can this be avoided?

- The items can be made three days after the order arrives if estimated production has already reached an intermediate process. The trouble with this strategy is that stocks increase and may become unusable if estimates are not accurate.
- Reducing the production cycle to within seven days will prevent missed delivery deadlines. Eliminating lot delays is one very effective means of achieving this.

Process Delays and Full Work Control

In the overall production cycle, the ratio of process delays to processing generally looks something like this:

Process delays		Processing time
80%	:	20%
60%	:	40%

It follows that eliminating process delays can shorten production cycles to roughly 20 percent of their current length.

Synchronization in two senses is an absolute prerequisite to dealing with process delays (see Figure 11-2):

1. The lots at each process following the process sequence must be of the same size, and processing times must be equivalent.
2. The timing of processes must match so that the entry of a part into one process exactly coincides with the completion of work at the previous station.

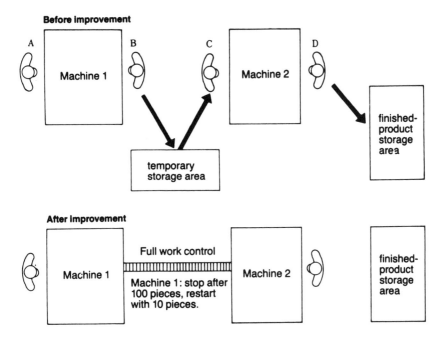

Figure 11-2. Synchronization and Full Work Control

We tend to assume that synchronization requires matching everything to the highest capacity machine in the process sequence. Since production volume need be no greater than required volume, however, synchronization may be attained by lowering the operating rates of high-capacity machines. To do this, we can set up a magazine to act as a cushion between, say, machine A (a high-capacity machine) and machine B and use the weaker machine to pace both A and B. The system might work like this:

- Machine A shuts down automatically when 100 pieces fill the magazine.
- Machine A starts running automatically when there are only 10 pieces left in the magazine.

As shown in Figure 11-3, this sort of arrangement, known as a "full work control system," can be adjusted very effectively to provide the constant control functions necessary to synchro-nize processes.

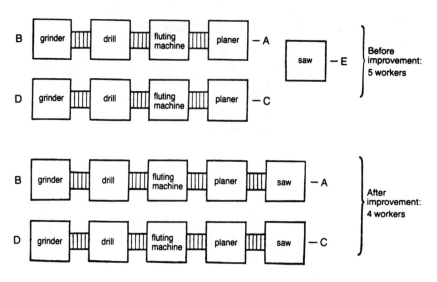

Figure 11-3. Machine Operating Rates Need Not Be High
(Example: A Woodworking Plant)

Lot Delays and Production Cycles

Now let us look at how to eliminate the lot delays we dis-cussed earlier.

Suppose we are conducting operations with lots of 1,000 pieces that go through ten processes. The production cycle can be defined as follows:

Production Cycle $L = T \times n = nT$
where $T =$ the processing time at one process
$n =$ the number of processes

If we use lot production and suppose that T equals five hours and n equals ten processes, then the production cycle can be calcu-lated as below:

$$L = nT = 5 \times 10 = 50 \text{ hours}$$

If we eliminate lot delays and institute one-piece flow operations,

$$\text{Production cycle } l = T \times (n - 1) \times t$$

where t equals the processing time for one piece, say 0.3 minute, which gives us:

$$= 5 \text{ hours} + (10 - 1) \times 0.3 \text{ minutes}$$
$$= 5 \text{ hours} \times 2.7 \text{ minutes}$$

Thus,

$$\frac{l}{L} = \frac{T + (n - 1) \times t}{nT} \approx \frac{1}{n}$$

$$= \frac{5 \text{ hours} - 2.7 \text{ minutes}}{50 \text{ hours}} \approx \frac{1}{10}$$

The production cycle can be reduced another 90 percent by cutting processing lots to one-tenth of their current size. An absolutely essential prerequisite for achieving this is the use of the SMED system to minimize setup times. (For further reading, see *A Revolution in Manufacturing: The SMED System* [Productivity Press, 1985].)

Dramatic Lead Time Reductions

So far, we have discussed three effects, as illustrated in Figure 11-4:

1. Production cycles can be reduced 80 percent by eliminating process delays and using full work systems to synchronize processes.
2. They can be cut 90 percent by eliminating lot delays.
3. They can be reduced another 90 percent by cutting processing lots to one-tenth of their current size.

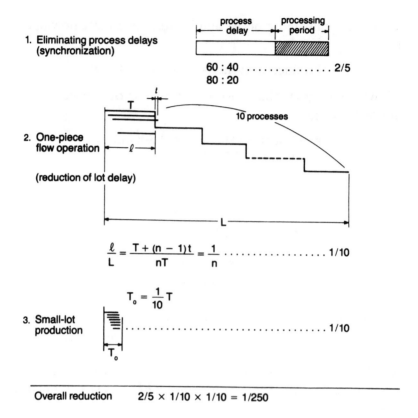

Figure 11-4. Dramatic Reductions in Lead Time

The sum of these effects shows that it is possible to achieve a dramatic reduction in lead times:

$$l = \frac{1}{5} \times \frac{1}{10} \times \frac{1}{10} = \frac{1}{500}$$

Using the example just given, a production cycle (= lead time) of 50 hours can be cut to 0.5 hour:

$$50 \text{ hours} \times \frac{1}{500} = 0.5 \text{ hour}$$

A real-life example comes from the Granville-Phillips Company in Boulder, Colorado. This U.S. company:

- cut production lead time from 4 weeks to 2 hours
- shortened a 1.5-hour setup changeover to 2 minutes
- abandoned anticipatory production and began producing only to firm orders in lots as small as ten pieces
- eliminated all finished goods inventories
- eliminated all transportation and inventory between processes by adopting a process sequence-based layout and one-piece flow operations

As a result of these improvements, Granville-Phillips cut labor costs by 60 percent and plant floor space by 40 percent. The company installed new equipment in the newly opened space and used the 60 percent labor surplus to manufacture new products. In the first year, the rise in productivity tripled profits. Profitability in the second and third years increased fivefold and in the third year the new product research budget was tripled.

All this was due to the active leadership and enthusiasm of Dr. Daniel Bills, the company's president and chairman of the board. One of my most trusted friends in the United States, he referred to me in his 1989 Christmas card as "my teacher and good friend."

12

The Improvement of
Process Control Systems

So far we have mostly discussed process improvement for single parts. Now we must consider the improvement of process control systems for assembly.

LARGE-LOT PRODUCTION AND
ANTICIPATORY PRODUCTION SYSTEMS

In terms of basic philosophy, I think it is fair to say that large lots and anticipatory (forecast-based) production underlie 90 percent of the world's factory production systems. As the phrase "cheaper by the dozen" suggests, large-lot production can reduce apparent labor costs because it spreads out the effects of setup times. On the other hand, large-lot production has the disadvantage of generating larger inventories. For this reason, scholars have come up with the idea of seeking an optimally economic lot size (Economic Order Quantity) that balances these two effects. But why didn't it occur to anyone to make drastic reductions in the setup times that lie at the heart of the "economic lot" argument?

I developed the single-minute exchange of die (SMED) system in 1969 in response to a request from Taiichi Ohno, the late former president of Toyota Motor Corporation. He wanted to cut the four-hour setup time on a 1,000-ton press down to one hour and then to three minutes. Indeed, recently we have achieved "one-touch exchange of die" (OTED) changeovers that are performed in less than a minute. The notion of an economic lot is unnecessary if we can shorten a four-hour setup to three minutes. In fact, large lot production becomes pointless.

Similarly, the only reason people have tried to deal with orders by using highly reliable forecasts is that production lead times have been longer than delivery cycles. For example, a production cycle might be twenty days when the delivery cycle is only five days. Inventory accumulation, considered to be an inevitable and necessary evil, is a drawback of forecast-based production as well. Stocks were tolerated at first and eventually regarded with indifference.

But what happens when we look at the factors responsible for excessively long lead times?

- Process delays of two hours, for example, can be cut 80 percent or more by synchronization.
- A shift from batch production to one-piece flow production can shorten lead times by over 90 percent. The resulting increase in transportation runs necessitates using process sequence-based layouts.
- Producing in drastically smaller lots has proved capable of reducing a lead time of four weeks to two hours.

Some scholars advocate "push" production systems, while others argue in favor of "pull" systems. Since production must by nature respond to orders, inventory in either case will always accumulate at intermediate processes when the production cycle (P) is longer than the delivery cycle (D). It follows that the idea behind non-stock production systems is that P must always be shorter than D.

Thus, fundamentals-oriented improvement paves the way for truly rational production systems — some of which we will now discuss.

FLOW SYSTEMS

The flow system, which made maximal use of the effects of the division of labor, has been seen as the first great revolutionary system of process management. Its consequences brought about the need for synchronization.

Henry Ford is usually credited with creating the idea of flow operations, but the record shows that Charles E. Sorensen actually set up the system. According to Sorensen, there was no place to put all the parts when an automobile was assembled in one place. Assembling auto bodies as they moved cleared up parts storage areas and improved efficiency. Sorensen, it seems, focused mainly on improving operational efficiency and did not intend to address the question of process improvement. No doubt this attitude was to be expected in an environment where production was seen as the performance of operations and where performing operations or tasks was thought to be all there was to production. He was surely satisfied by the unprecedented rise in productivity brought about by the effects of the division of labor.

Sorensen never dreamed that his innovation was rooted in process-based improvement and surely did not realize how many other improvements would follow it. In fact, having given birth to many process systems, flow operations became the basis for all assembly methods.

USING CLUSTERED SYSTEMS

Machine Assembly

It is not at all uncommon to go to a factory's assembly area and see a small number of workers, say fifteen people each, lined up and assembling parts for Companies A, B, and C. Ask why things are arranged this way and you will be told the plant wants to avoid complaints from visiting representatives of Companies A, B, and C who worry that parts might not be delivered on time if they don't see people working on their orders.

Suppose the plant explains to its customers, however, that their delivery deadlines will be strictly observed for the following reasons:

- From the first to the tenth of the month, forty-five people will finish Company A's order.

- Company B's order will be produced between the eleventh and the twentieth of the month.
- Company C's order will be finished between the twenty-first and the thirtieth of the month.

This arrangement means the company will meet Company A's deadline of the tenth and Company B and C's deadlines on the twentieth and the thirtieth, respectively. It also means reduced inventories and a roughly 10 percent efficiency improvement due to the simplification of individual tasks. This approach, in fact, always improves productivity.

Depth Gauge Assembly

I was once transferred from a railway plant in Taiwan to become plant manager at Company M, a Yokohama manufacturer of depth gauges. Because Company M was unable to meet its production targets, I conducted a survey of the situation. I found it was the inability to achieve targets in body production that led to missed delivery deadlines for all finished parts.

I was told that a 20-centimeter post in the center of the 25-centimeter pan-shaped base of the body made it necessary to machine the parts on large 8-foot lathes. The fact that there were only five such lathes available made the lathe operation a significant bottleneck.

A detailed examination of the process revealed that 6-foot — or even 4-foot — lathes were capable of machining some of the parts. However, I was told they couldn't be used because excessively small end plates made parts impossible to mount.

Having special large end plates made to accommodate the bodies and then using a total of twenty 6- and 4-foot lathes to run a one-piece-at-a-time flow operation allowed us to produce the bodies in ten days. We then removed the large end plates from the twenty lathes and ran medium-sized and small parts. The result — we doubled productivity within two months. I called this system "short-term flow operations," but the idea is exactly the same as a clustered production system.

Consolidating Roadwork

I have noticed that work on roads and highways often holds up traffic and inconveniences people because it is performed by relatively few people working at a number of different sites simultaneously. I believe there would be fewer long-term interruptions and less inconvenience if large numbers of workers were concentrated at a few key sites. This would enable them to complete the work in a short period of time and also significantly improve the efficiency of the work. Why haven't the authorities thought of a clustered system that would promote both public convenience and roadwork efficiency? I hope those responsible for public works reflect on the question.

PROCESS-BASED SYNCHRONIZATION SYSTEMS

Synchronizing Processes and Enhancing Capacity

Running a system of flow operations always requires synchronization. In particular, when trying to implement a flow system with multiple lines, many people think it difficult to set up comprehensive process-based synchronization to handle different assembly families. This belief, however, is based on a widespread misconception. Indeed, much of the problem fades when the problem is approached analytically.

The first thing to understand is that the volume produced should be exactly the same as the volume required. Most managers run into all sorts of difficulties because they think they have to synchronize all other machines to the highest capacity machine. But if the daily output required is 5,000, there is no reason to try to bring the capacity of all the machines up to 6,000 pieces per day just because the machine with the highest capacity can process 6,000. Machines that can handle 5,000 pieces a day can be left the way they are.

Sometimes, of course, a machine with a capacity of 4,500 pieces per day will need to be synchronized at the 5,000-pieces-per-day level. The most effective approach would be to improve the capacity of the machine. In situations where raising capacity is difficult, however, a second machine will have to be added.

Building Inexpensive In-house Machines

When the addition of a low-operating rate machine cannot be avoided, the machine should be constructed in-house and inexpensively. Depreciation, we should remember, eventually makes machines free, but wages must be paid to workers indefinitely.

Mr. Yamamoto, the head of manufacturing at Fukushin Denki Company (Eiji Miyauchi, president) near the city of Himeji, is an enthusiastic proponent of in-house machine construction. A 300-ton press costs $52,000 on the open market, but Mr. Yamamoto's group built one in-house for $16,000. The plant also built for $6,000 a bending machine that would have cost $20,000 had they bought it from outside.

Constructing machines in-house allowed Fukushin Denki to limit itself to providing functions that were necessary and sufficient for its specific purposes and to suppress any extraneous functions. It was able, for example, to make the head and flywheel by welding, paying close attention only to the final finishing process to ensure that proper balance was achieved.

In another instance, when it came time to add a bias cutter at B Tire Company, they modified some old drawings imported from the United States. While the original machine could cut material from large bolts of fabric, B Tire's version could handle only the medium-sized bolts used in current operations. Adhering to the original design would have cost the company $800,000, but B Tire built the machine for $320,000 — less than half the cost.

These companies eliminated the costs of underwriting an outside manufacturer's risk and profits by reviewing machine functions and redesigning machines themselves. Parts were made by specialty firms, but the assembly work was done in-house. The results were substantial cost reductions.

Advantages of In-house Fabrication

Generally speaking, machines can be made at one-third the market price by matching machines to the needs of synchronization and by eliminating the following cost components:

1. extraneous functions
2. "idea" costs
3. profits
4. risk charges (such as for rework)

In addition, synchronization based on the assumption that production volume must equal required volume can prevent the accumulation of inventories and can bring in significant profits even if machine operating rates are low.

Many people assume that the goal of rational production is to increase machine operating rates. A broader view of the problem is needed, however — one that weighs the benefits of higher operating rates against the losses incurred by burgeoning inventories. Indeed, from this perspective, a serial synchronization system may not pose such insurmountable problems after all.

Slowing Down Sewing Machines

Most of the sewing machines at A Company, a firm that sews automobile car seats, run at 3,000 rpm. The company achieved significant results by specially ordering some low-speed 1,700-rpm machines and intentionally put them into the line. Capacities were matched with other machines, cushion stocks no longer had to be made and kept in the line, and efficiency improved by roughly 15 percent. The new arrangement made it possible to work with less expensive machines, and it cut breakdowns because reduced wear of rotating parts meant easier maintenance.

We often assume that mechanization means we have to run machines 100 percent of the time. But do we?

Processing Television Cabinets

The N Company is a woodworking concern located in the city of Takayama. Because it was using a batch production approach with machines laid out according to equipment type, I proposed an improved one-piece flow arrangement for producing television cabinets, in which two lines would be dedicated, respectively, to the manufacture of large and small cabinets. I asked Mr. Ohmizo, the plant manager, to automate a number of processes, including cutting the product (saws), surface planing (planers), channel cutting (planers), cutting windows (routers), and grinding (sanders). I also recommended the automation of handling operations such as turning the products over and around and transporting them from one process to the next.

When I visited again two months later, the plant had, indeed, organized the machines through sanding operations into lines. Because there was only one circular saw for the initial cutting process, however, the machine was running alternating batches for large and small cabinets and creating work-in-process in the interim. The machine would batch process materials for a certain number of large cabinets, stoppers would then be changed to match the dimensions of the smaller cabinets, and the machine would run a certain number of the new sized materials.

When I asked Mr. Ohmizo why he didn't install saws in both lines, he told me such an arrangement would be wasteful because the machines' operating rates would then be too low.

At that point, I went to the company's president and told him I had asked his plant manger to set up two continuous lines from cutting to sanding. He replied he had heard of my recommendation and explained why they had decided to stay with one saw. The cutting operation, he said, was such a simple one that the saw's operating rate was less than 40 percent even when it was running both families.

"All right," I replied. "How much does a saw cost?"

"Probably about $1,875.

"In that case," I said," how about buying another one and setting up two independent lines from cutting to sanding? This means a workpiece for the large cabinet will flow automatically all the way through to final sanding as soon as worker A cuts the raw board. The same thing will happen on the small cabinet line with worker C, so you eliminate the need for one worker — worker E.

"This new arrangement," I added, "will get rid of in-process stock, eliminate wasted manhours, and shorten the production cycle. It's true the operating rate of the saw will drop, but your profits will go up!"

"You're right!" Mr. Ohmizo exclaimed. "The problem isn't that the apparent machine operating rates go down — it's which approach is the most profitable."

The improvements were put into effect without delay. They are shown in Figure 12-1.

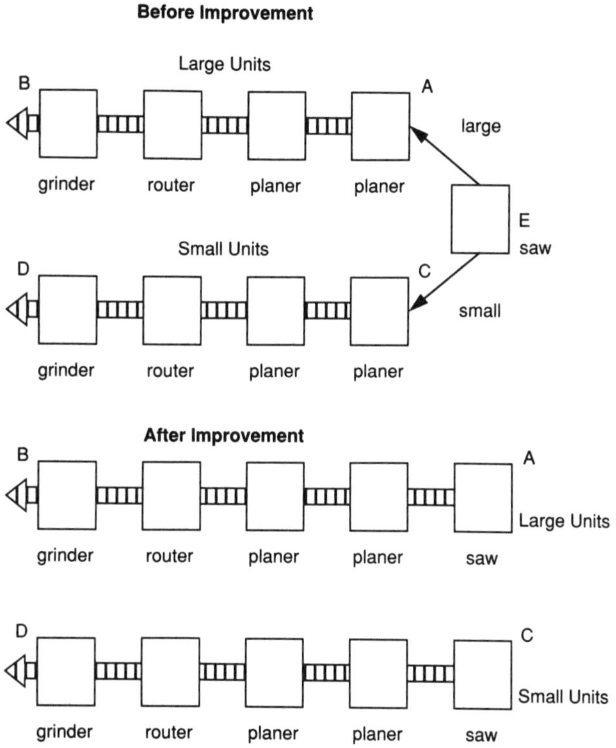

Figure 12-1. Improved Layout for Processing Television Cabinets

Executives and managers often pursue nothing more than short-sighted gains in machine operating rates. The real issue is profits, however, and while increased operating rates may raise profits, operating rates are not necessarily the real problem.

Indeed, they are a second-order issue and it is important to understand clearly that profits can often be raised even when operating rates fall.

MIXED MODEL PRODUCTION

Electronics and other fields have recently seen a growing demand for small volumes of a large variety of products. At the same time, there is a growing awareness that it is profoundly illogical to deal with such demands by using mass anticipatory production and accumulating large inventories.

Mixed model production systems provide a way out of this apparent contradiction. By mixed model production, we mean continuously assembling three products — P, Q, and R, for example — in combinations proportionate to their demand.

Changeovers will unavoidably generate considerable idle time if the *takt* times (or what the market is demanding) for P, Q, and R vary significantly and if changeovers are carried out at the same time. With mixed model production, however, changeover losses disappear because different models are assembled together. Let us suppose, for example, that each of the products requires twenty process steps and that their respective *takt* times are as follows:

1 P: 2 minutes

- Q: 1.5 minutes

1 R: 1 minute

In this situation, changing over the entire line entails major time losses:

- Changing from P to Q generates a loss of 10 minutes (2 minutes − 1.5 minutes × 20).
- Changing from P to R generates a loss of 20 minutes (2 minutes − 1.0 minutes × 20).
- Changing from Q to R generates a loss of 10 minutes (1.5 minute − 1 minute × 20).

Recent trends toward high-diversity, low-volume production result in more frequent changeovers and effectively multiply these losses. Companies will end up being squeezed if they attempt to minimize inventories in the face of demands for a wide array of low-volume products.

When *takt* times increase, changeover losses can be staved off temporarily by having a foreman or team leader help out. In the long run, however, this strategy is not particularly effective.

And this is where mixed model production comes in. Whether you are dealing with large product lots or individual units, setup losses are the same — the issue is the relative merit of producing a steady stream of a single item. It turns out to be more advantageous to increase the number of changeovers.

An approach that allows us to do this includes the following elements:

1. Devise common jigs and fixtures to reduce setup labor costs to zero.
2. Use Zero Quality Control or ZQC (that is, a system of source inspections and mistake-proof *poka-yoke* devices) to eliminate all instances of missing or mistaken parts.
3. Handle items with relatively longer *takt* times (P and Q in our example) by having operators follow the flow of the products.

The advantage to be gained is that the production process can be synchronized at an eight-minute cycle by making units in a mix reflecting the demand; for instance, $1 \times P : 2 \times Q : 3 \times R$.

In any event, there are two crucial points we must not forget:

1. We must minimize setup losses.
2. ZQC (source inspections and mistake-proof *poka-yoke* devices) is an absolute necessity for eliminating all cases of missing or mistaken parts resulting from product differences.

We need to see smaller lots, demands for an increasingly varied bill of fare (product assortment), and inventory elimination as underlying constraints on production. Indeed, demand governed by such constraints is becoming more and more prominent.

This sort of mixed model production needs to be flexible enough to be able to respond immediately to changes in the product mix. Achieving such resiliency is by no means easy; if possible, the wisest strategy is probably to handle the problem with flexible machine operating rates.

A mixed model production system also involves shifting from a conventional "static" parts supply system to a dynamic one in which turntables or similar devices are used to feed needed parts to the line when they are needed and only in the amounts needed.

In addition, increasing the frequency of supply runs from parts stores to the line is important. The labor costs of assembling and transporting assembly parts need to be reduced, allowing workers to concentrate on assembly tasks.

BLOCK PRODUCTION

The Block Assembly of Ships

In 1956 I worked at Mitsubishi Heavy Industries' Nagasaki Shipyards to shorten the time it took to build the 650,000-ton supertanker Independence. Supertanker hull construction at that time took ten months in England, seven months in West Germany, and four months in Japan. By dividing tasks according to welding skill requirements, we set a world's record by shortening that time initially to three months and then to two months. The factor most responsible for the short construction cycles of Japanese ships was the use of a "block construction" system pioneered by Captain Yomogidani of the Kure Navy Yard.

The block construction system consisted of dividing the hull into 400 (80 bow-to-stern and 5 port-to-starboard) separate blocks and building the blocks inside sheds. The block approach contrasts with conventional, out-of-doors construction in several ways:

- Block construction eliminates disruptions to welding operations caused by rain.
- Blocks are assembled in parallel rather than sequentially.

- Block sizes ranging from 30 to 50 tons mean that the only work carried out in the yard is the mating of one block to another.

The dramatic shortening of the construction cycle through parallel block assembly and the successful elimination of disruptions to welding caused by rain should be seen as a revolutionary improvement. The assembly cycle was significantly compressed by dividing the hull into manageable blocks, assembling individual blocks in parallel, and then mating the blocks in the dry dock berth only at the end of the process.

Vulcanizing Pan Production

In one case, the sequential assembly of parts for an automobile tire vulcanizing mold used to take forty-two days. We improved this process so that the mold was broken down into several blocks, individual blocks were processed in parallel as much as possible, and then the blocks were assembled. Within six months, we reduced the processing time to four days.

Leveled Production

It goes without saying that production is easiest when task loads are leveled out with respect to one another. But a distinction must be made here between "external" and "internal" leveling.

External leveling refers to level demand, a situation entirely dependent on demand-side fluctuations over which the producer exercises no control. In principle, the producer has no choice but to respond to demand fluctuations with flexibility in capacity.

The Y Company, for example, has found several measures to be extremely effective:

- Regular eight-hour shifts are punctuated by four-hour gaps between the day and night shifts. Demand peaks are handled by using these four-hour periods for overtime work, thereby increasing capacity by 50 percent.

- Further increases in capacity are obtained by having indirect workers help out with deburring and other simple tasks.
- Assistance is sought from suppliers able to provide it.
- Pre-automation measures allow nighttime operations. One or two workers stay on duty to handle minor machine breakdowns, while major breakdowns await repair on the regular shift.
- Layout improvements shorten the production cycle so recovery can be achieved during the order cycle.

Whatever approach is chosen, flexible capacity provides the optimal response to demand fluctuations.

Cushion Stock Systems

Many factories temporarily warehouse parts from suppliers and then deliver those parts to the line in response to requests from assembly processes. Shop floor managers at such plants typically show uneasiness and strong resistance to the suggestion that parts be delivered from suppliers' plants directly to the assembly line.

In a situation like this, a rethinking of traditionally slighted process functions needs to lead to a major evaluation of all production functions — especially process functions. The following steps might be taken:

1. Retain a certain amount of inventory in the warehouse and designate it "cushion stock."
2. Have suppliers deliver parts directly to lines in the assembly plant.
3. Draw from the cushion stock to cover a certain level of late deliveries or defects. Replenish the stock the following day.

As it eliminates uneasiness and clarifies — in quantitative terms — how much cushion stock is really needed, the cushion stock approach leads to speedy resolution of delivery and quality problems and to a smooth and gradual shift toward a system in which parts are delivered directly to the line. Increasing attention will be focused on any irregularities that do arise and prompt corrective measures will deal with defects, blunders, or other problems.

Plants with no prior experience of direct line-side deliveries can use this cushion stock approach with great effectiveness.

THE SUPERMARKET SYSTEM

This is a system using minimal inventories to handle situations in which production cycles and production volumes cannot deal with demands for immediate delivery.

The idea is that appropriate quantities of product are stocked and production replenishes only what is withdrawn for delivery to customers. Minimal sizes for these stocks can be determined by balancing two sets of factors:

- customer demand frequency
- customer demand volume

and, on the production side:

- production speed (lead time)
- rapidity of setup changeovers
- flexible capacity to handle loads (how quickly and to what extent can loads be adjusted?)

Some scholars argue that this approach only increases inventories because it is based on estimates. In fact, however, stocks are held to a minimum because the shop floor produces items only to replace those that have been sold. If an item is not sold, it is not produced.

The "supermarket" approach allows the Toyota Production System to respond to demand fluctuations with a minimum of stock. In this sense, it embodies the just-in-time (JIT) system.

Used in the restaurant industry and other businesses where immediate delivery is crucial, this method enables companies to make massive reductions in expected inventories of defective products. The most important prerequisites to the supermarket approach are probably:

- lead time minimization

- small-lot production and one-touch changeovers
- elastic capacities

MULTIPLE MACHINE HANDLING
AND MULTIPLE PROCESS HANDLING

Multiple machine handling refers to a situation in which, for example, an operator does nothing but load and unload workpieces for several of the same type of gear cutting machines. An example would be a situation in which a human worker loads and unloads machines with long automatic processing times because the automation of those functions is difficult or offers poor returns on investment.

In multiple process handling, by contrast, machines are laid out according to the processing sequences, and the human operator transports, unloads, and loads workpieces in that same sequence. Multiple process handling often accompanies a one-piece flow system. One-piece flows can shorten lead times dramatically, but they have the disadvantage of increasing the frequency of transport runs.

The correct approach to improvement is to devise a system of pre-automation and enhance return on investment by finding low-cost methods to move, unload, and load parts.

As we have seen, improving processes is a critical first stage of process control enhancement. Only when process improvements alone cannot do the job should we seek to supplement them by improving operations. It is important to keep this point in mind: starting out with facile operational frills is a mistake.

Part V

The Second Function of Production Management: Operational Improvement

Up until now, efforts to improve production functions have concentrated solely on upgrading the functions of operations. We need to see and understand this bias more clearly.

13

Process Functions and Operational Functions

We have already emphasized that production is a network of processes and operations. The first thing we need to ask is what series of process steps is involved in making the product — what functions, in other words, transform raw materials into finished products. Next, we turn our attention to operations (or tasks), such as secondary functions that actually form the product, along with the temporal and spatial streams in which people work on physical objects.

Process functions take precedence over operational functions, but recognition of the former takes place mostly inside the heads of process designers. Most people have difficulty recognizing what process functions are in concrete, visual terms. Process functions tend to be overlooked, moreover, because their dispersed movement around the factory gives them poor visibility. Operational functions, on the other hand, are repeated over and over again in fixed locations where the actual status of the product can be verified. Under the circumstances, it is not surprising that people have made the mistake of believing production to consist of nothing but operations.

A correct understanding of production activity functions, however, requires that we never forget the necessary sequence of steps leading to improvement: examine process functions thoroughly and then consider supplementary operations (see Figure 13-1).

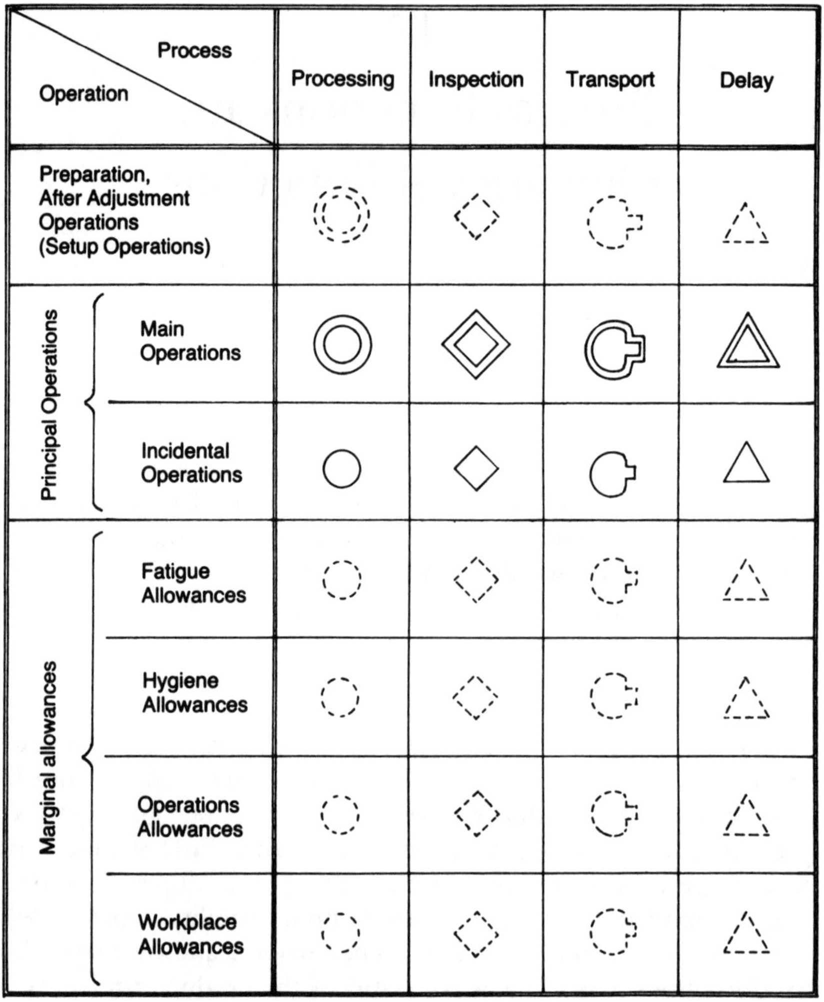

Process / Operation	Processing	Inspection	Transport	Delay
Preparation, After Adjustment Operations (Setup Operations)	◌	◇	◖	△
Principal Operations — Main Operations	◎	◈	⬤◖	◬
Principal Operations — Incidental Operations	○	◇	◖	△
Marginal allowances — Fatigue Allowances	○	◇	◖	△
Marginal allowances — Hygiene Allowances	○	◇	◖	△
Marginal allowances — Operations Allowances	○	◇	◖	△
Marginal allowances — Workplace Allowances	○	◇	◖	△

Figure 13-1. Production Mechanisms

That said, the question of how we improve operational functions is obviously extremely important, given the fact that such functions are the ones responsible for actually making the product.

It was the discovery of the principle of the division of labor in England in the 1750s that clearly separated two functions that until that time had been fused in the bodies of individual workers:

- processes — flows transforming raw materials to finished products
- operations — flows in which people perform work on physical objects

Process functions were spread out among machines all across the shop floor and consequently imposed themselves very little on people's awareness. An operation, on the other hand, in which a machine in a fixed location would process a thousand parts, one after another, made a strong appeal to the perception of repeated actions that actually make products. The result was that people ended up believing that production and operations were equivalent.

Careful investigation of the nature of production, however, reveals two different agencies at work. The "conceptual" effect of the process sequence — such as asking what the most efficient order of processes is — takes precedence. This is followed by the "supplementary" effect of operations, or existential tasks. The problem was that the conceptual effect took place in the mind of a specific process designer and could not be observed objectively by other people. Few perceived it, therefore, and the impression left by the widely recognized existential effects of operational functions ended up being all the more vivid. The conceptual action of determining a process sequence — the absolutely essential prerequisite to operational effects — was slighted and forgotten for roughly 200 years.

In 1921, Frank B. Gilbreth clearly pointed out the existence of process functions in production — functions comprised of four phenomena: processing, inspection, transportation, and delays. But he placed process and operational functions on the same axis, explaining that processes were the result of analyzing production into large units of analysis and operations were determined by analyzing production into small units. The difference between processes and operations, he claimed, was only one of the size of analytic units. Gilbreth failed, in other words, to recognize that "process" is an independent production function.

Finally, in 1945, I pointed out clearly that production is a network of orthogonally intersecting processes (the Y-axis) and operations (the X-axis). Processes are flows by which raw materials become products, and operations (which supplement processes) are flows in which people perform work on items one after another at each process. This was the first time the notion of process was accorded full consideration.

I argued that we should first establish the process sequence and then determine effective operational methods to supplement that process sequence. Improvements in process functions have a profound impact on operational functions. Some operations may be eliminated and some may be radically changed. Figure 13-2 presents an overview of my perspective.

A great deal of publicity has been generated about the Toyota Production System, but the crucial issue does not lie in the superficial features of the system. We need to recognize that the correct way to view the Toyota system is to see it as a production system emphasizing processes — a production system based on my new concept of production as a network of processes and operations.

By merging the new SMED and OTED concepts with minimal lot sizes and 99 percent reductions in lead times, the Toyota Production System has successfully created a "non-stock" production system that has raised profits three to five times their previous levels.

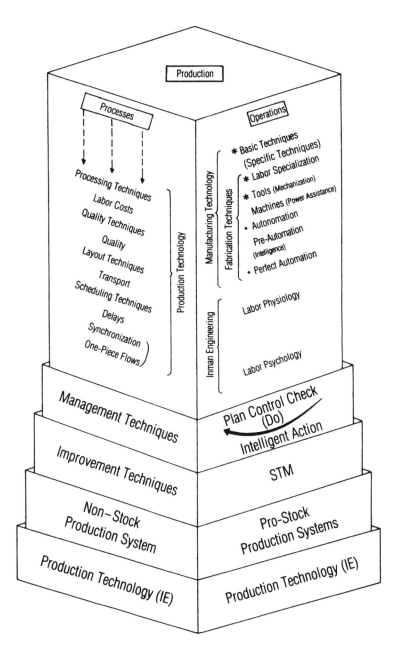

Figure 13-2. Manufacturing Technology and Production Technology

14

The Effect of the Division of Labor
on the Development of Work

The appearance of the division of labor in England in the 1750s had a revolutionary impact on work productivity.

At once an advance in labor psychology and labor physiology, the division of labor increased productivity in a number of ways, as illustrated in Figures 14-1(a) and (b). Some examples:

1. Eliminating the element of decision from simple repetitive tasks made movements almost reflexive and allowed tasks to be performed quickly.
2. Simplifying motions facilitated their "mechanicalization" and, with the subsequent addition of power, rapid mechanization. Mechanization increased productivity substantially and led to "autonomation" (jidō ka) or "automation with a human touch," which provided machines with sensors and such that give them cognitive functions. This development further reduced the scope of human intervention and once again increased human productivity.

   Total automation would need to both detect abnormalities and correct them, but restoring things to a normal state is generally quite difficult. The development of the concept of "pre-automation," in which sensors detect abnormalities and humans correct them, led to a dramatic reduction in human work.
3. Intermediate motions involved in picking up and putting down tools were eliminated.

4. The repetition of simple movements meant tasks were learned more quickly.
5. The subdivision of skills meant that more people could perform work, and employment opportunities increased. Unemployment fell substantially, and an invigorated society grew rich as most prices fell and goods became more lavish.
6. Sustaining quality became easier, and the operating rates of tools and machines rose.

England's industry grew rapidly and the nation prospered as her ships brought colonies under her control throughout the world. Further significant gains in efficiency were won by applying the division of labor to machines as well as to human work.

Despite its success, the division of labor was not without drawbacks:

- It made human work monotonous and tiresome, and brought about local fatigue in certain muscles and joints used more than others.
- It relied on cooperative efforts, so that the failure of one part of the system could have a devastating impact on the whole.
- The need for overall balance called for consideration of planning and control issues.

The merits of the division of labor far outweighed its disadvantages, however, and the principle was applied in every kind of production activity.

| Stone/Wood Hand Tools – Hand Power | | Metal Hand Tools – Hand and Animal Power | | Mechanical Tools – Mechanical Force and Electricity |
First stone tools developed (500,000 B.C.)	More modified tools (50,000 B.C.)	Bronze Age (6,500 B.C.)	Iron Age (3,400 B.C.)	Industrial Revolution (1830–)
Pounding	stone wood	stone ball hammer (Egypt)		steam hammer (Naismith - England 1839)
Drilling	stone-tipped awl	bow awl (Egypt) chisel		drill (England 1840) horizontal boring machine (England 1775)
Chipping	polished stone hand axe	hand axe (Egypt)		planer (England 1817)
Splitting	polished stone hand axe	bronze axe		wood splitter
Pulling and Cutting	wooden sickle sharp stone blade	saw (Egypt)		band saw (France)
Slicing	hard stone blade	bronze knife	knife	lathe (England 1800)
Polishing	polishing tool polished flintstone	polished ball	file	grinder (1880)
Attaching	leather thongs	bronze nail	rivets caliper metal ruler	electric welding (1886)
Measuring	physical length (18"– 22")	stone ruler (Egypt)	caliper	micrometer (1887) Vernier caliper

Figure 14-1(a). The Evolution from Hands to Machines

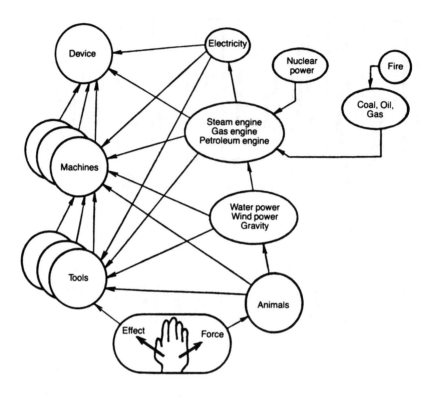

Figure 14-1(b). The Evolution from Hands to Machines

15

Types of Operations

Operations (or tasks) may be categorized as shown in Figure 15-1.

SETUP IMPROVEMENT AND
THE DEVELOPMENT OF SMED

Changing from one operation to the next inevitably requires a shift of procedures known as a "setup change." Strictly speaking, setup changes lie outside the domain of operations. Standing like a formidable mountain at the intersection of operations and processes, setup changes have been a major impediment to the progress of both, and the only road over the mountain pass has been an arduous one.

The traditional solution was to minimize per-item costs by keeping as much inventory as possible and reducing the number of trips over the pass. There were disadvantages, however. The fact that this approach required vast storage space and diminished return on investment led to the development of the idea of economic lot sizes. In the meantime, there were attempts to make the work of transport as easy as possible, to smooth out steep curves and pave the road surface. In developing the idea of the "single-minute exchange of die" (SMED) setup, I blasted a tunnel through the mountain, so to speak — dramatically shortening the

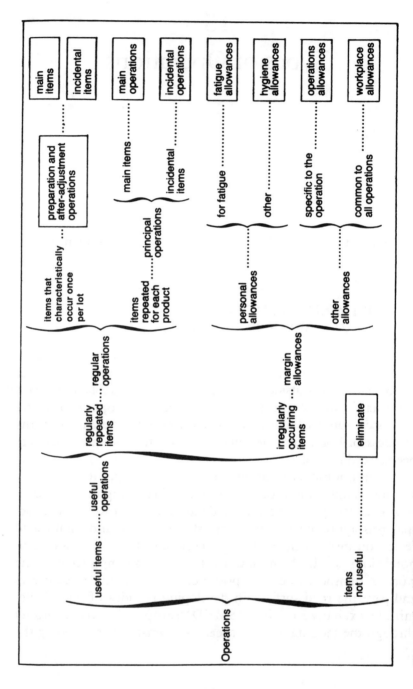

Figure 15-1. Types of Operations

time it took to move between processes or operations. Cutting four-hour setup changeovers to three minutes simply blasted out of existence the band-aid approach of economic lot sizes.

The SMED concept itself evolved in three stages.

Step 1

In 1950, I watched a setup changeover on a large press at Tōyō Kogyō (now Mazda) in Hiroshima. Finding himself short one bolt at one point, the worker performing the changeover wasted considerable time cutting to size a longer bolt he had scavenged from another press nearby. Seeing this, I realized that machine operating rates could be increased dramatically by making a clear distinction between two essentially different kinds of setup elements:

- *Internal setup elements* are setup tasks that absolutely require that the machine be shut down.
- *External setup elements* are setup tasks that can be performed while the machine is running, either before or after internal setup.

External setup should be carried out while the machine is still running. Internal setup should be performed only while the machine is shut down.

Step 2

In 1956, I witnessed setup changeovers carried out in the production of diesel engines at Mitsubishi Heavy Industries' Hiroshima Shipyard. Here, the practice of placing engine beds on a planer table for centering and marking off lowered the machine's operating rate considerably. We raised that rate 40 percent by constructing a second table for centering and marking off while the machine was still running. The actual setup changeover consisted only of exchanging one table-and-bed unit for another.

Step 3

In 1963, a setup changeover on a 1,000-ton press at Toyota Motor (Toyota City, Aichi Prefecture) took four hours to complete. At the same time, however, Volkswagen in Germany was doing the same setup in two hours. We spent half a year trying to overtake them and finally reduced the setup time to an hour and a half. When we went to see the plant manager one morning, he then ordered us to cut the changeover time to three minutes.

My immediate reaction was that it was impossible, but then I had a flash of inspiration. It dawned on me that the Mitsubishi Shipyard's planer improvement had involved shifting to external setup elements that everyone had assumed had to be part of internal setup. On a nearby blackboard, I immediately wrote out eight ideas for improvements designed to move as many internal setup elements as possible to external setup. Then, with the help of two first-rate Toyota engineers (Messrs. Ikebuchi and Ohta), within three months we reduced the setup time to three minutes.

To this day, I believe SMED would never have come into existence if it hadn't been for plant manager Taiichi Ohno's utterly unreasonable directive to reduce the setup changeover to three minutes.

Taiichi Ohno's View of SMED

Taiichi Ohno wrote the following account for the Japan Management Association's journal *Management* in June 1976:

> Up until ten years ago at Toyota, we used to produce as much as we could during regular hours and then change cutting tools and bits and so forth during the noon break or after work at night. Even during the last ten years of rising production, we often used to push our tools to the limit because we didn't want to take the time to change the tools — even when we were supposed to change tools every fifty pieces. It takes a lot of time to change all the many cutting tools and bits on equipment like a transfer machine. On a multigrinder, for instance, it takes about half a day, and on a Wednesday this would mean shutting down production all afternoon. So, we tried having people come in on Sundays to do it — but that cost too much money. We also

wanted to do all maintenance during regular hours, so everybody studied up on how to make changeover times very short.
Shigeo Shingo, who used to be with the Japan Management
Association, advocates making setup changeovers in less than ten
minutes. It used to take us half a day to make a changeover so
that we could do ten minutes' worth of manufacturing. When
setup changes take half a day, you want to spend at least that
much time producing, so you end up making a lot of things you
don't even need. Now we have people working on setup
changeovers that last only a few seconds — which is easy enough
to say but hard to accomplish. One way or another, however, we
must shorten setup times.

In his book *The Man Who Built the Toyota Production System*,
Wataru Noguchi writes:

> ...even so, Ohno's insistence that a setup change that used
> to take hours be slashed to three minutes was of a difficulty that
> transcended common sense. This is how Ohno describes what he
> had in mind: "Shingo had already reduced a four-hour
> changeover to an hour and a half for us. Therefore I thought he
> might be able to get it down to three minutes if I asked him."
>
> Ohno's account seems to reflect a bit of arrogance — or
> did he really expect Shingo to be able to do it? He may have
> been the one who asked Shingo to come up with a three-minute
> setup changeover, but Ohno probably didn't think it could really
> be done. He most likely figured that anything under ten minutes
> would be a success. Three months later, when three minutes was
> finally achieved, Ohno was the first to rejoice over the feat. The
> reason was simple — setup times had to be shortened drastically
> if just-in-time production was going to work, and up until then
> the unresolved setup problem had blocked the whole system.

In the final analysis, there are three points to keep in mind
when implementing SMED. They are illustrated in Figure 15-2.

1. Setup changeovers consist of two essentially different kind
   of elements: internal setup and external setup. Drawing
   this distinction clearly is the first crucial step.
2. All tasks traditionally assumed to have been carried out in
   internal setup should be re-examined and internal setup
   elements should be shifted to external setup.

3. Each component task of both internal setup and external setup needs to be improved thoroughly.

Persistent improvement of this type at Koga Kinzoku (Yukio Koga, president) in Fukuoka Prefecture has resulted in a press changeover that takes less than fifty seconds. Moreover, the setup is automated — all the operator has to do is push a button.

Changeovers on thirteen 75-ton presses at San'ei Kinzoku Kōgyō (Hiroshi Kondō, managing director) in Kumamoto Prefecture are not "single-minute" setups as much as they are "one-touch" setups. With the next die lined up in front of each press, activating the start switch automatically releases the clamps securing the old dies, which are then pulled out with magnets and air cylinders. Other air cylinders push in the new dies and they are automatically clamped in place. All thirteen presses can be changed over in a mere fifty seconds (see Photo 15-1).

My book *A Revolution in Manufacturing: The SMED System* has been translated into many languages, and editions have appeared in the United States, France, Italy, Spain, Sweden, Finland, Yugoslavia, Brazil, and Australia. Applied to production activities all over the world, the ideas it contains constitute a powerful weapon for revolutionary increases in productivity. Even in Japan, I suspect the Toyota Production System would never have achieved such effectiveness were it not for the SMED concept.

OPERATIONAL FUNCTIONS

Process functions consist of processing, inspection, transportation, and delay. There are corresponding operations or tasks for each, and each operation is accompanied by setup changeovers.

Operations can be divided into "main operations" and "marginal allowances." These can be broken down further as follows:

$$\text{main operations} \left\{ \begin{array}{l} \text{primary operations} \\ \text{incidental operations} \end{array} \right.$$

Main operations do most of the work of translating corresponding process functions into action.

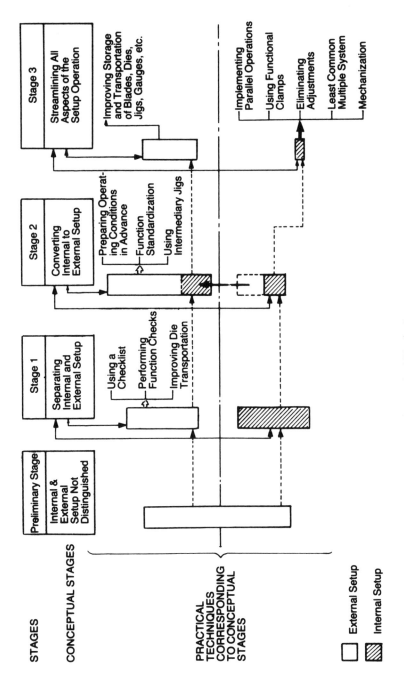

Figure 15-2. SMED: Conceptual Stages and Practical Techniques

Photo 15-1. Managing Director Hiroshi Kondō and the San'ei Kinzoku Kōgyō plant that successfully changed over thirteen presses in fifty seconds.

Primary operations, which characteristically require specific technological expertise, might include:

$$
\text{marginal allowances}
\begin{cases}
\text{personal allowances}
\begin{cases}
\text{fatigue allowances} \\
\text{hygiene allowances}
\end{cases} \\
\text{other allowances}
\begin{cases}
\text{task allowances} \\
\text{shop allowances}
\end{cases}
\end{cases}
$$

- actual processing or machining
- altering shape (cutting, forging, casting, etc.)
- altering state (quenching, annealing, etc.)
- assembling (fitting together, welding, plating, etc.)
- disassembling (breaking down by electrolysis, etc.)

Comparable technical skills are needed for inspection, transportation, and delay operations:

- inspection — basic skills for comparing items with standards
- transportation — basic skills for changing locations
- delay — main operations here must involve technical skills called for by delays (periods during which no processing,

inspection, or transportation takes place), as well as placement considerations (level and three-dimensional storage, rustproofing, anti-oxydation measures, etc.)

Incidental operations supplement primary operations and are composed of such tasks as loading, unloading, attaching tools and fixtures, removing, centering, and measuring.

Marginal allowances are tasks that take place sporadically when regular main operations are not being carried out. They are supplementary to main operations and their purpose is to allow main operations to be carried out smoothly:

- "Fatigue allowances" are allowances for rest breaks, and so forth to recover from operation-induced fatigue.
- "Hygiene allowances" are allowances for fulfilling physiological needs, such as going to the bathroom, drinking water, and wiping away perspiration.
- "Task allowances" are allowances for wiping away chips and adding cutting oil, lubricants, and so forth.
- "Shop allowances" are allowances for machine maintenance (such as for repairing machines that have broken down and for assuring the timely arrival of materials).

Improvement in tasks such as these should aim at removing the need for human involvement: human labor can be saved as mechanization proceeds, and measures can be taken for such tasks as chip removal mechanization and preventive maintenance.

In the final analysis, fundamental improvements must address the sources of abnormalities.

THE MECHANIZATION OF MANUAL FUNCTIONS

We can divide human hand motions into two types: (1) transport motions and (2) work motions. The advent of the division of labor greatly simplified work motions while "mechanicalization" transferred most of these motions to tools.

The next move was to augment the power of the human hand. People first used animal power and then moved to power sources found in nature, such as water, wind, and gravity. The identification of fire as a source of power led, in succession, to coal, oil, and atomic power as the discovery of fuels made it possible to provide rich sources of energy. A new problem arose, however — that of "transporting" energy. It was here that the discovery of electricity revealed a power source that was both convenient and effective. In recent years, researchers have discovered an extremely efficient means of transmitting energy in superconductivity.

Such "artificial" power has given rise to a host of deleterious side effects. Carbon dioxide emissions, for example, have brought about a deterioration of the earth's environment and made the development of "clean" energy sources all the more pressing. From the viewpoint of the future of the human race, the solution clearly lies in the further study and development of energy present in the natural world. Examples include:

- solar light and heat, the ultimate source of all energy
- storms
- the energy in wind, water, gravity, and oceanic currents and waves
- disparities in the temperature of the earth and the oceans

In any event, the addition of power to human hand motions resulted in a mechanization that massively transferred human labor to machines.

THE AUTOMATION OF MANUAL FUNCTIONS, OPERATIONAL IMPROVEMENTS THROUGH ROBOTIZATION, AND "PRE-AUTOMATION"

The mechanization of primary operations has been accompanied by innumerable advances in research and development. Some examples are the invention of blades for cutting and the subsequent development of new cutting tools and the discovery of cutting methods; Taylor's invention of high-speed steel; the invention of diamond cutting tools; and the development of various welding methods, precision forging, precision casting, electro forming, and wire cut methods. Similarly, improvements in incidental operations have included the mechanization of product loading, unloading, and turning; the mechanization of machine activation and shutting off (such as the use of machining centers); and the mechanization of numerical control (NC) and multidimensional processing (such as programs for NC machines and for computer support).

After mechanization came "autonomation" *(jidō ka)*, the provision of machines with human intelligence. Autonomation means providing machines with sensor functions and the dual capacity to detect abnormalities and to restore normal operations. Because detecting abnormalities was easy compared to recovering from abnormalities, total (or "perfect") automation did not spread very much. As a result, I advocate a "pre-automation" system, in which sensors automatically detect abnormalities and humans resolve the problem. Used primarily in process industries, autonomation has spread throughout machine, equipment, and other industries. It has enabled numerous human tasks to be transferred to machines and has contributed massively to saving energy.

Nonetheless, some human motions remained despite the progress of mechanization and autonomation. These have been absorbed by two developmental tracks of robotization: "task robots" and "intelligent robots."

Mechanization, pre-automation, and robotization will no doubt continue to progress unabated. We must never lose sight, however, of the crucial need for prior process improvements.

TPM AND SKILLS MANAGEMENT

As people gradually attempt to transfer human work to machines, they expect those machines to run smoothly without abnormalities. Preventive maintenance (PM) can be seen as a focused attempt to make this possible.

If the idea of transferring work from humans to machines is a major path to progress, then PM must be a high-level objective for the efficient conduct of production activities. Although some people argue that PM is a panacea for all aspects of production, it seems to me that, while some PM may have a tremendous impact on some aspects of production, there are other areas in which PM would have little effect in making production more efficient. In any case, the PM approach to production is a passive one and should be seen as such.

In contrast to PM, "skills management" should be seen as a more active approach in the sense that it more effectively exploits latent machine functions. While skills management attempts to draw out 100 percent of latent machine performance, an even more aggressive approach can be seen in the idea of making machining unnecessary; for example, doing all processing at once of parts that are now processed piecemeal or by precision casting or precision forging.

We have already seen that Total Productive Maintenance (TPM), or PM applied on a companywide basis, is the name given to comprehensive campaigns for promoting PM activities. If basic PM functions and practices are not up to par, however, the most important effect will be gained by studying ways to improve them.

IMPROVING HUMAN NATURE

No matter how much human labor may be mechanized, autonomated, and robotized, there will always remain some tasks for people to perform. In the realm of management, too, it will no doubt be impossible to eliminate people altogether. It ultimately follows that we must pay attention to the problem of human nature. In 1960, McGregor claimed that there were two aspects to human nature: Type-X and Type-Y characteristics.

With the opening up of the North American continent in the late 1800s, many new pioneers sailed to the United States. Factories and industries were set up and many people were hired. However, while people of that era had experienced work, they were as yet unaccustomed to laboring for wages, particularly when the work did not suit them. Capitalists and managers concluded that workers were lazy and that they were not people so much as providers of labor. Given this perspective, they developed labor practices in which they were quick to lay off workers when there was no work to do and to rehire them when business picked up. The resulting employment instability led U.S. workers to form a national labor union in 1866, and the "class struggle" began.

DEALING WITH HUMAN NATURE

This trend eventually gave birth to socialism and communism, and probably led to the considerable instability in the world. The world would no doubt be a different place if labor and management had built harmonious relations in the early 1800s instead of opposing one another. It is a sad fact that the decision that workers were basically lazy is one of the great misjudgments of human history.

Type-X and Type-Y characteristics coexist in all of us; other external factors determine which of the two gains the upper hand. While I believe that religious faith and education are influential factors in promoting Type-Y characteristics, I wonder how many people realize what a weighty responsibility should be borne by modern educators in Japan? Figure 15-3 depicts a breakdown of Japanese and Western influences on production systems.

The so-called "Volvo System" that appeared in Sweden in 1968 shocked the world by advocating the abandonment of conveyors, but the Volvo approach is superficial. It simply strikes a compromise with Type-X characteristics and pays no attention to the improvement of human nature by refining Type-X into Type-Y characteristics.

THE PACK SYSTEM

Many companies have gotten excellent results by applying the pack system. While this system improves work methods, it should also be seen as a means of providing people with goals and instilling high levels of motivation that draw out their latent abilities.

Management by objectives and zero defect campaigns are other types of motivational systems. I believe that even greater advances can be achieved when these systems are applied in concert with policies that get to the heart of human nature by refining and promoting Type-Y characteristics in human beings.

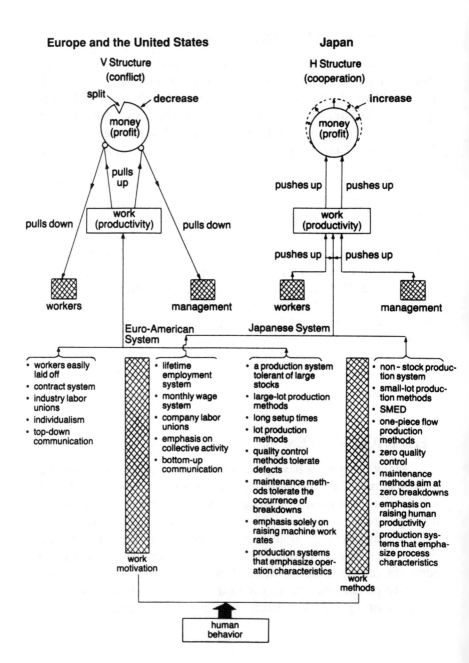

Figure 15-3. How Human Nature Is Treated in Japanese and Western Production Systems

Part VI

Basic Steps to Improving Productivity

16
How to Raise
Productivity Worldwide

A visual presentation of the procedures discussed so far for deciding on a production system is shown in Figure 16-1. The following circumstances can be seen as the principal steps taken to raise productivity throughout the world.

1. THE DISCOVERY OF THE DIVISION OF LABOR (1750s)

As we have said many times, the division of labor was a truly revolution discovery in the development of modern industry. As shown in Figure 16-2, it led — and brought rapid progress — to later developments such as mechanization, autonomation, and robotization.

2. DEVELOPMENTS DUE TO MECHANIZATION, AUTOMATION, AND PRE-AUTOMATION

The discovery of the division of labor greatly facilitated mechanization. With the provision of elements of intelligence, automation became "autonomation." These developments resulted in massive savings in strictly human labor and in increased productivity.

Procedure for establishing a production method

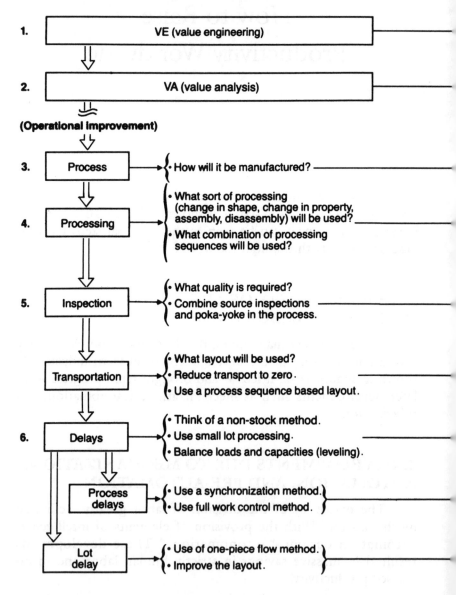

Figure 16-1. Procedures for Deciding on a Production System

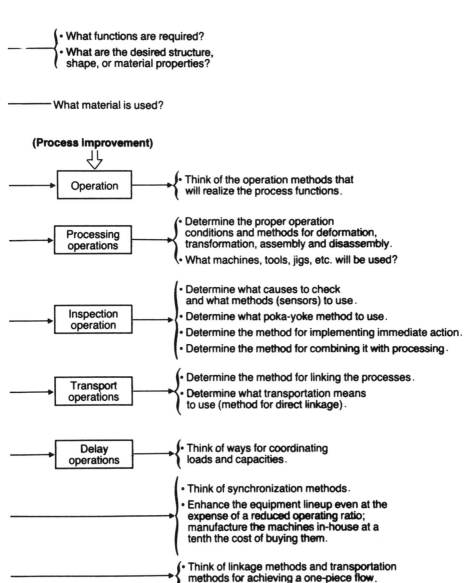

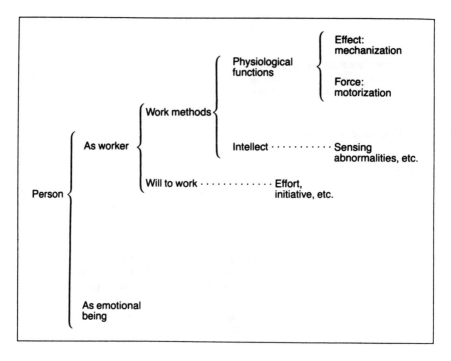

Figure 16-2. Human Functions

3. A MORE EFFICIENT CONTROL FUNCTION IN MANAGEMENT

Activating the control function of management activities makes it possible, for example, to achieve zero defects.

4. THE SCIENTIFIC STUDY OF WORK

Around 1883, attempts were made in the United States to enhance worker motivation by using contract work systems. Output rose sharply, prompting those who held the capital to conclude that the unit prices used as standards were too high. They cut the unit prices. After a while, workers recovered from their discouragement and began working harder. Output again shot up and unit prices again were slashed. The result — more discouragement.

When this cycle had repeated itself a number of times, workers came to feel they would be exploited no matter how hard they worked. They began "soldiering" — a term for organizational sloth — and used labor unions to restrict the volume of work because anyone who worked too hard would drive unit prices down.

This was the year in which Frederick W. Taylor became a foreman. He realized that soldiering impeded the development of U.S. industry and asked the crucial question of whether it served the cause of the workers' personal happiness. Feeling the answer to be an emphatic "no," Taylor looked into the causes of soldiering and concluded that the culprit was vague work standards.

If standards were conceived more scientifically, he reasoned, there would be no need to be so quick to lower them. He analyzed work into small component tasks and set scientific standards based on thoroughgoing studies of those individual tasks. He advocated a previously unimaginable combination of high efficiency, high wages, and low costs — and increased productivity dramatically by achieving all three.

5. GILBRETH'S CREATION OF THE IDEA OF IMPROVEMENT

In observing the work of bricklayers around 1885, Frank B. Gilbreth began to question common assumptions about significant individual variations in the speed of work. While he had vaguely expected that variations could be traced to differences in experience, it occurred to him that perhaps different work methods were the cause. He devised a system of motion elements called "therbligs" that he used to conduct detailed studies of work. From these studies, he derived that the difference in performance lay in differing motions and work conditions. He then showed that improving the motions and conditions of the work of inexperienced bricklayers allowed them to generate the same output as experienced workers. Gilbreth concluded from this that "time is simply a reflection of motion" and that focusing on resultant time and urging workers to work faster was of no use. The only way to improve the situation, he argued, was to improve the motions responsible for slow times. We can paraphrase Gilbreth by pointing out that defects, too, are a reflection of motion.

The myriad motions people make differ only in the objects they hold in their hands. Gilbreth argued that only eighteen therbligs are needed to describe hand motions and that the functions of those therbligs are constant. This perspective, he indicated, facilitates improvement. Using this approach, Gilbreth promoted what he called "motion studies." He also encouraged improvement by asking *"why?"* at least three times in the pursuit of goals and pointed out that there may be multiple means to a single end. His search for "ideas for means" led him to advocate the current "one best way" of performing a given task.

Gilbreth's most important contribution was his emphasis on the relentless pursuit of goals.

6. THE SCIENTIFIC THINKING MECHANISM FOR IMPROVEMENT

In my view, the pursuit of goals — or ends — takes place in three dimensions:

- X: looking for goals behind what you think the goal is now
- Y: looking for multiple goals that constitute the goal you see now
- Z: looking for a "real" goal above the goal you see now

I have also described the transformation of goals into means. By this, I mean that what we now believe to be a goal is nothing more than a means to some higher-order goal and that this goal is a means to a still higher-order goal. Because goals are linked to one another in this sort of chain reaction, our pursuit of goals needs to be relentless, sequenced, and oriented toward fundamental causes.

Dr. Ken´ichi Horigome gave me a thorough grounding in this teaching of Gilbreth's in Tokyo in 1937. The lessons I learned then later gave birth to such ideas as the SMED system, "Zero" Quality Control (the system that eliminates defects using source inspections and mistake-proof *poka-yoke* devices), and the Nonstock Production System.

I feel strongly that a thorough appreciation of Gilbreth's ideas is absolutely essential when attempting to raise productivity, whether in Japan or in the United States. An overview of my ideas on the evolution of production systems is presented in Figure 16-3.

7. HUMAN NATURE AND THE HAWTHORNE WORKS EXPERIMENT (1927)

The Hawthorne Works was the site of experiments conducted to judge the effects of lighting on work efficiency. When researchers gradually raised the level of illumination, output gradually rose. Surprisingly enough, however, output continued to rise when the level of illumination was gradually lowered. Unable to explain their results, the researchers turned to psychologists who explained that work output was influenced by psychological as well as physical factors. The lesson was that significant attention had to be paid to human factors in production.

The Hawthorne Works experiment marked the discovery of Type-Y traits. Later developers of Management by Objectives and zero defect campaigns, however, did no more than use these traits. It never occurred to them to make the fundamental improvement of changing Type-X into Type-Y characteristics.

8. THE VOLVO SYSTEM MERELY COMPROMISES WITH TYPE-X CHARACTERISTICS

In a book titled *People at Work: Surpassing the Ford System*, Volvo president Pehr Gyllenhammar advocates the elimination of conveyor lines. Gyllenhammar's argument was to address the monotony and oppression of assembly-line work in a country where human nature is tending toward Type-X traits and where the motivation for working is receding in the face of the high tax burden borne by Swedes to support their country's extensive welfare apparatus. But why didn't it occur to Volvo to take measures to transform Type-X into Type-Y characteristics? I am told that taxes in Sweden have risen again recently, a trend that in the future will surely lead the country down a slope of gradual decline.

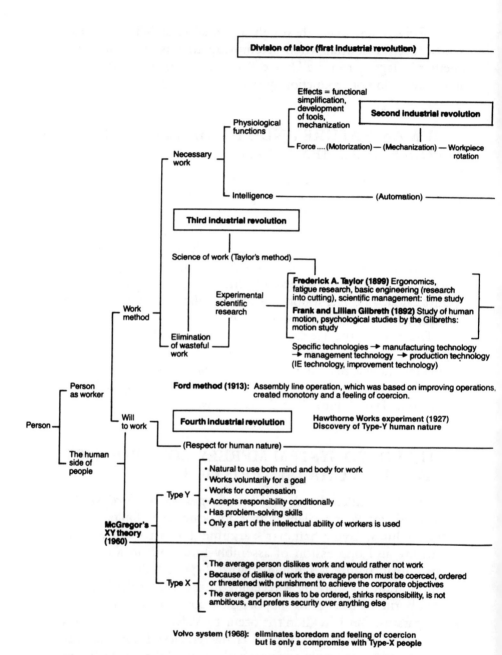

Figure 16-3. The Evolution of Production Systems

———————————— **Adam Smith: *Wealth of Nations* (1776)**

– Cutting — Installation/ — Replacement — Machining — Numerical — (Mechanization — Program — Computer — Robots — Intelligent
  blade   removal of   of cutting tool   centers   control   of assembly)   control   control   robots
  feeding workpiece   (dedicated   (NC
                         machines)   machines)

——— Detection of ———————————————————————————— Detection and correction
     abnormalities-(pre-automation)   of abnormalities
                                                           (perfect automation)

                         |

     (Developed by Shigeo Shingo: 1969)

"Time is the shadow of motion"

———————————— (Use of management by objectives and ZD movement)

**Responding to Type-X people: pay-by-results plan, quick layoffs and development of
radical, adversarial labor unions and class struggle**

**Responding to Type-Y people: day-rate plan, lifetime employment, cooperative company unions,
easy promotion of circle activities and total activities**

Gyllenhammar writes about "surpassing the Ford system," but the Ford system represented an improvement in production work methods. The Volvo system, on the other hand, is an approach that addresses work motivation. Gyllenhammar's premise is therefore completely off-base and his argument simply illusory. Wouldn't Volvo do better to reflect on why it is 2.7 times less efficient than Japanese companies in producing cars?

9. A CORRECT UNDERSTANDING OF PRODUCTION ACTIVITY MECHANISMS

The advent of the division of labor in England in 1750 was the dawning of productivity increases throughout the world. Although the division of labor clearly separated process functions and operational functions that until that time had been fused in the work of individual workers, people recognized only operations. For some 240 years, they dismissed the process functions that were, in fact, necessary precursors of operational functions.

It was while conducting an improvement survey at Hitachi Ltd.'s Kasama plant in 1945 that I realized clearly that production is a network of processes and operations. I reported that conclusion at a Japan Management Association technical conference and published an article on the same subject in *Production Standard Data*.

I have opened each of my books since that time with a description of the network structure of processes and operations, and constantly stress the point in my lectures. I emphasized process improvement to over 6,000 managers and engineers in roughly 100 production engineering seminars at Toyota between 1955 and 1980. The results are visible in the Toyota Production System, which rose to world prominence because of its tremendous resiliency in the face of the first shock of the oil crisis in the 1970s. Dubbed the *kanban* system, after one of its characteristic methods, or the just-in-time (JIT) system, the Toyota approach has been publicized around the world.

The creation of the SMED system was the key factor enabling the Toyota Production System to overcome its biggest bottleneck: setup time reduction. It is what made the explosive growth of the Toyota system possible. At the same time, productivity improved dramatically and profits increased many times over because Toyota adopted methods such as the following:

- the "Zero" Quality Control system and the achievement of zero defects through source inspections and mistake-proof *poka-yoke* devices
- drastic lead time reductions (from four weeks to two hours) due to the use of "one-piece flow" production accompanied by layout improvements
- the total elimination of inventories through the use of non-stock production systems

Part VII

Improving Productivity
in the Future

Is it really necessary to conduct comprehensive reviews of current production management systems based on an understanding of basic production management improvement steps?

17

Final Thoughts

WHERE DO WE GO FROM HERE?

Productivity improvements have a history spanning many years. Which way should Japan head as it continues to improve production management? Let us try to predict some directions for future progress.

1. Relentlessly pursue processing-related improvements in order to improve overall processes. Ground-breaking improvements are needed here, as serious studies have so far been few.

2. "Zero" Quality Control: source inspections, mistake-proof *poka-yoke* devices, and the implementation of prompt corrective measures will bring about zero defects. Sensor developments and advances in the prevention of inadvertent errors will considerably reduce machine stoppages.

3. Layout improvements will eliminate transportation although some small-scale transportation will remain between machines. Either such transportation should be minimized or inexpensive transport mechanisms should be developed.

4. Synchronization methods for eliminating process delays will become increasingly ingenious and reliance on "full

work" systems will no longer be necessary. Integrated one-piece flow systems running from parts processing to assembly will be implemented to eliminate lot delays.

5. Setup improvements will move from SMED (under ten minutes) to "one-touch" (OTED) changeovers carried out in seconds. There will also be a shift from remote control to automatic changeovers. Programmed automatic setup changes will take place even during unmanned night operations made possible by pre-automation.

6. Among process phenomena, increasingly sophisticated technical developments in the improvement of processing and in primary processing operations will lead to advances in processing technology.

7. High-level technologies will be developed for incidental operations.

8. In terms of human allowances, sophisticated pre-automation will decrease human intervention and eliminate the need to think about tasks.

9. The continuous improvement of fundamental phenomena will eliminate nonhuman shop and task allowances.

Developments such as these will maximize the transfer of production shop work from people to machines. Clean energy sources will be developed as well, and methods will be devised for providing energy from solar heat and light and from other natural phenomena. Figure 17-1 shows the transition to a non-stock production system, and Figure 17-2 outlines the Toyota Production System from an industrial engineering perspective.

IMPROVEMENT FOR THE FEELING HUMAN BEING

So far, we have discussed issues relating to people as laborers. However, we also must make improvements relating to people as emotional human beings.

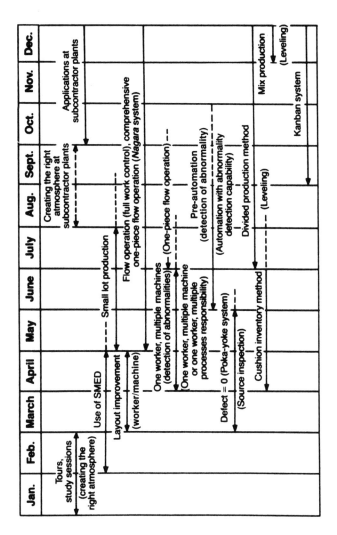

Figure 17-1. The Transition to a Non-stock Production System

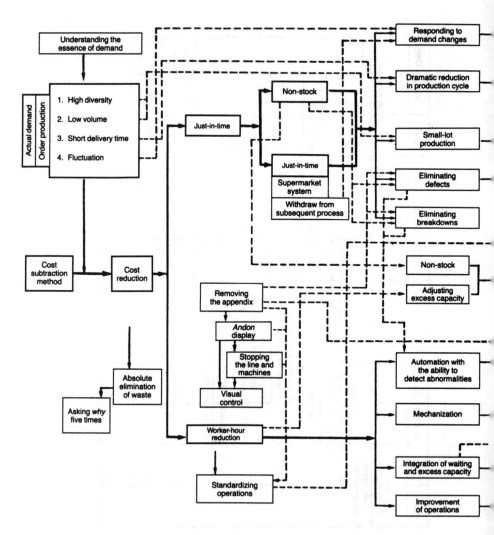

Figure 17-2. The Toyota Production System from an Industrial Engineering Perspective

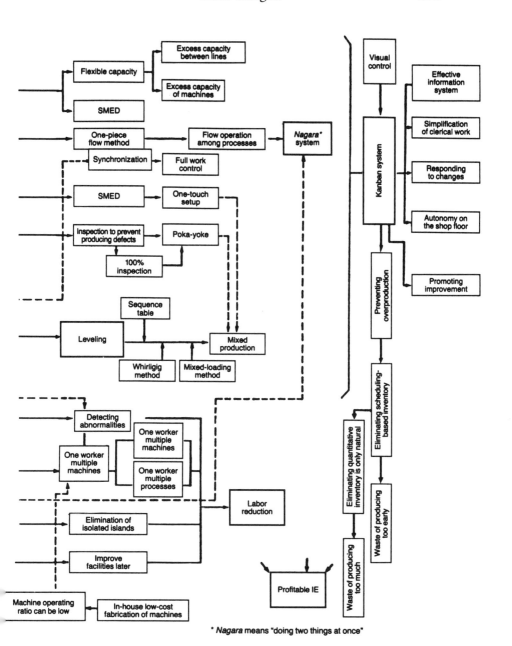

* *Nagara* means "doing two things at once"

First, we must change Type-X into Type-Y characteristics. In order to do this, mandatory retirement systems and measures to stabilize employment should be accompanied by at least threefold wage increases, the quarterly disbursement of incentive pay based on profits, and employee shareholder programs. Mutual antagonism must be replaced by harmony.

As horizontal equality eliminates glaring disparities in basic social levels, vertical equality will stimulate the individual to work by compensating capable people in accordance with their efforts.

Freedoms of speech, thought, and religion must be guaranteed, and tyranny and oppression banished.

The saying "man does not live by bread alone" is ironic in that bread is an absolute physical necessity without which no one could exist. The phrase means that bread is not enough, however. We also need food for the spirit.

To achieve this, we need to increase food production, reclaim deserts, and expand the practice of agriculture. At the same time, we need to streamline production in primary industries much more than we need to develop distribution or information industries. We must increase productivity at least three times to make that happen.

I would like to see a thirty-hour work week — six hours a day, five days a week — become reality within the next five years. I envision starting a workday that runs from 7:00 to 11:30 in the morning and then, after a lunch break, from 12:10 to 2:40 in the afternoon. Time after work would be spent pursuing hobbies or sports, or with the family.

Isn't it preferable for people to spend more time as feeling human beings with lives rich in family, friends, and service? A major factor in its realization, I think, will lie in changing Type-X to Type-Y characteristics.

Dominant Type-Y characteristics constitute the basic reason for Japan's high labor productivity. Japan is extraordinarily poor in natural resources. Indeed, Japan has nothing but high quality labor supported by a high level of education, circumstances that sustain a harmonious relationship between labor and management. If Type-X traits were allowed to persist, Japan would decline in short order.

This is why Japan has adopted a system of lifetime employment, why wages are comparatively high, and why freedom of speech is guaranteed. Japan as a modern economic superpower is founded on liberalism and democracy. Regrettably, however, certain unorthodox educators and myopic scholars, managers, and politicians have recently lost sight of this basic perspective. What can they be thinking, I wonder, as they try to lead Japan into ruin?

TWO SIDES OF HUMAN NATURE: LABOR AND EMOTION

Human beings are at once "creatures of labor" in a production context and "creatures of emotion" in their social lives.

As we have already mentioned, people have always labored on their own initiative for survival — to provide themselves with food, clothing, and shelter. Things changed, however, when they were put into a situation where, in order to receive wages, they had to work even if they disliked the task. The antagonism between labor and capital led to the creation of labor unions, collective organizations formed to counterbalance owners and managers. Since owners, for their part, saw workers as mere providers of labor, they forced them to accept low wages and did not hesitate to lay them off. All this gave rise to massive disparities of wealth in the working class.

Communism and socialism arose as attempts to close this gap. Governments eliminated unemployment, guaranteed wages, and took other measures so that all people could live in equality. Extravagant welfare systems were implemented in an attempt to guarantee universal equality. But how are these systems paid for? In Sweden, the income of a worker who has just graduated from middle school is reportedly taxed at 35 percent, and I am told the rate has recently increased. On one visit to Sweden to consult for an automobile company, I was asked many questions by a vice president in charge of production who was unusually enthusiastic about improving the plant. At lunchtime, I asked him how much he paid in income tax.

He responded, "Please don't ask. When anybody brings up the subject of taxes, I lose interest in working."

"Then why are you asking so many questions?" I asked.

"Because the whole country will end up going down the drain if we don't think about revitalizing this plant," he answered.

He finally told me that he was taxed at about 85 percent of his income.

Some commentators describe Sweden's welfare system as perfect, but can you imagine how the Japanese would react if they were asked to pay an 85 percent income tax? In Japan, political parties and citizens clamored for a change of government over a paltry 3 percent sales tax! I am persuaded by recent world events, moreover, that the kind of equality offered by socialism and communism is nothing but equal poverty.

Communism is said to have achieved the limited — although undeniably lofty — goal of guaranteeing universal equality. But seventy years of history have shown that equality to be one of poverty, of a dearth of food and material goods. The recent emergence of *perestroika* in the Soviet Union and the move away from communism in the Eastern Bloc countries are, I think, a reaction to that fact. It may be true that no more people are starving, but communism and socialism have fostered a kind of "horizontal equality." No one seems to have given much thought to a "vertical equality" in which people who are more capable and who work harder are rewarded for their Type-Y traits. So what has happened? By a kind of Gresham's Law, bad labor has driven out the good. Society's ranks have swelled with Type-X people who only produce at the low level of initiative still tolerated by the community as the productivity of the overall country deteriorates. At Volvo, worker motivation is extremely low, opportunities for improvement are everywhere, and operations seem slack. Productivity is 2.7 times worse than in Japanese automobile factories. One can hardly expect productivity to rise in a country where someone can quit a company and then wait until unemployment insurance benefits run out before getting a new job.

Capitalist nations guarantee unemployment protection through welfare systems, but there is a tendency for recipients of such welfare to demand unemployment compensation as a right and to forget that such benefits are a favor bestowed by those who are working. Increasingly, those who demand pensions include people who are still healthy, and not just single mothers, the infirm, and the aged who are truly needy. We must point out how unreasonable it is for governments to accede to such demands.

Despite the lip service paid to the equal distribution of wealth in communist and socialist countries, many among the abler and more industrious people have seen their own new ideals systematically quashed. Given the suppression of their freedoms of thought and religion, moreover, it seems to me the current upheavals in Eastern Europe and the Soviet Union are due to their people's quest for liberation and escape from inferior living standards. No fundamental change will take place without a guaranteed affluent standard of living — and this ultimately means an absolute need for increased productivity. When all is said and done, we must correctly understand the phenomena discussed in this book and then proceed to carry out production in the most efficient way possible.

In any event, I cannot overemphasize the importance of having one point etched clearly in our minds: we can never expect to have a prosperous nation or a contented citizenry unless we increase productivity.

In the final analysis, national prosperity depends on improved productivity and, conversely, it is only on a foundation of increased productivity that we can build a wealthy nation and happy citizens.

No expansion of tertiary industries can ever bring about true national prosperity because such industries are merely decorative — like idle blossoms.

And doesn't the ultimate solution to the recent chaos in Eastern Europe and the Soviet Union need to be fashioned out of increased productivity?

I can only deplore the current situation in which Japanese politicians — for unknown reasons — seem not to share these perspectives.

Afterword

As I finish this book I have the impression of having devoted too much space to discussing the division of labor. Indeed, the subject appears three times in the table of contents. I hope readers will indulge me in this, however, because the division of labor was the starting point, the wellspring, of all modern improvements in production management.

There are a couple of other themes I have stressed over and over, perhaps to the point of tedium:

- Be aware of process functions in production management!
- Reorienting human nature toward Type-Y characteristics is a fundamental issue.

The Toyota Production System is built on pioneering concepts that give a central role to process functions. I emphasize the points above because people seem content to treat the Toyota system like just another production system and to mimic its external attributes without trying to understand and study the essential concepts behind it.

In the United States, serious studies of these ideas are underway at M.I.T. and other universities. I am even told that a condensed version of my books — *Modern Approaches to Manufacturing Improvement: The Shingo System* (Productivity Press, 1990) — is being used as a college text. The contrast with the response in Japan is alarming.

I feel a certain dissatisfaction as I look at my concluding chapter and wonder how close I have come to fulfilling my over-ambitious intention to provide a focused and comprehensive explanation of production management functions.

Unlike my other books, in which I have dealt with individual systems, this has been my first experience in attempting to capture all the functions of production management and explain each of them. How will readers react? I don't know. I await their response with a mixture of 70 percent apprehension and 30 percent hope.

On further reflection, I cannot help feeling that people have not thought rigorously enough about the notion of improvement.

Another thought: Why is it that Gilbreth's ideas about making work more rational attracted so little attention in his own country? Even in Japan, I have the impression that the idea of efficient thinking is thought to be out-of-date, a not particularly highly regarded relic of classical industrial engineering. Yet I believe this particular element of Gilbreth's thinking to be the mother of improvement and progress. Why do people think so little of it? Efficient thinking is the true parent of a number of creative production systems such as:

- SMED
- systems of source inspections and mistake-proof *poka-yoke* devices
- drastic lead time reductions
- non-stock production systems

Trade friction between Japan and the United States has once again become an issue. Regardless of how much political weight is flung about, however, I cannot see finding any real solution to the problem unless America adopts the right production management methods and begins exporting true quality products at low cost. And then what will happen? Japan will quickly slide toward a ruinous abyss unless it makes serious efforts to raise productivity further still.

Having long since arrived at the twilight of life, I have raced against time in my desire to leave this book to posterity. Little by little, I put pen to paper over the course of many a cold winter's day, and I now savor the profound satisfaction of having finished in time. This, I believe, will be the last of many books in which I have presented new ideas to the reading public, and it seems a fitting occasion now to acknowledge the readers with whom I have shared my journeys in this world. Once again, I offer you my sincerest gratitude for supporting me throughout these many years.

Finally, for the ordeal they endured to bring this book to publication, I would like to express my heartfelt thanks to Kazuya Uchiyama and Eiko Shinoda of the Publishing and Information Division of the Japan Management Association. For the English versions of my books, I warmly thank my American publisher, Norman Bodek, president, and the staff of Productivity Press.

> This is probably the last book I will ever write, and though I am loath to leave the many memories it evokes, I present it, with affection, to my wife.

Appendix

A DEVELOPMENTAL GENEALOGY OF MANAGEMENT THOUGHT ON THE CRITERIA FOR THE SHINGO PRIZE

Year	Major Publications and Events
1750	Division of labor started in England
1776	Adam Smith discusses division of labor in *The Wealth of Nations*
1797	Robert Owen uses modern labor and personnel management techniques in a spinning plant in the New Lanark Mills in Manchester, England
1798	American inventor Eli Whitney manufactures guns using interchangeable parts
1813	Robert Owen, *A New View of Society*
1814	Owen makes observations on the effect of manufacturing in his *Two Memorials on Behalf of the Working Classes*
1821	Scottish economist James Mill, *Elements of Political Economy*

1829	English mathematician Charles Babbage designs "analytical engine," anticipating modern digital computer
1832	Babbage, *On the Economy of Machinery and Manufacturers*
1833	Factory law enacted in the United Kingdom; formation of early labor unions in the United States
1835	American Samuel Morse invents the telegraph
1839	Opium War begins between China and Great Britain
1857	International recession spreads to the United States and Western Europe
1861-1865	U.S. Civil War
1866	Sir William Siemens invents electrical generator
1869	Transcontinental railroad completed in United States
1876	Alexander Graham Bell invents a usable telephone
1877	Thomas Edison invents the phonograph
1878	Frederick W. Taylor joins Midvale Steel Company
1880	American Society of Mechanical Engineers (ASME)
1883	Taylor begins time study
1885	Frank B. Gilbreth begins motion study
1886	Henry R. Towne presents paper, "The Engineer as Economist"; American Federation of Labor (AFL) is organized
1888	Frenchman Henri Fayol joins top management team of Commentry-Fourchamboult mines
1890	Sherman Anti-Trust Act enacted in the United States
1892	Gilbreth completes motion study of bricklaying
1893	Taylor begins work as consulting engineer

1895	Taylor presents paper titled "A Piece-Rate System" to ASME
1898	Taylor begins time study at Bethlehem Steel; Taylor and Maunsel White develop process for heat-treating high-speed tool steels
1899	Carl G. Barth invents slide rule for calculating metal cutting speed as part of Taylor system of management
1901	American national standards are established; Yawata Steel begins operation
1903	Taylor presents paper titled "Shop Management" to ASME; H.L. Gantt develops the "Gantt chart"; Hugo Diemers writes *Factory Organization and Administration*
1904	Harrington Emerson implements Santa Fe Railroad improvement; Thorstein B. Veblen, *The Theory of Business Enterprise*
1906	Taylor establishes metal-cutting theory for machine tools
1907	Gilbreth uses time study for construction
1910	Gantt establishes the Gantt award program
1911	Taylor, *The Principles of Scientific Management;* Gilbreth, *Motion Study;* factory laws enacted in Japan
1912	Harrington Emerson, *The Twelve Principles of Efficiency;* Frank and Lillian Gilbreth present the concept of "therbligs"; Yokokawa translates into Japanese Taylor's *Shop Management* and *The Principles of Scientific Management*
1913	Ford uses belt conveyor in assembly
1914	World War I begins; Clarence B. Thompson edits *Scientific Management,* a collection of articles on Taylor's system of management

1915	Taylor's system is used at Niigata Engineering's Kamata plant in Japan; Robert Hoxie, *Scientific Management and Labor*
1916	Lillian Gilbreth, *The Psychology of Management;* Taylor Society established in United States
1917	The Gilbreths publish *Applied Motion Study*
1918	Mary P. Follet, *The New State: Group Organization, the Solution of Popular Government*
1919	Gantt, *Organization for Work*
1920	Merrick Hathaway presents paper, "Time Study as a Basis for Rate Setting"; General Electric establishes divisional organization
1921	The Gilbreths introduce process-analysis symbols to ASME; Washington naval limitation treaty
1922	Sakiichi Toyoda's automatic loom is developed
1924	The Gilbreths announce results of micromotion study using therbligs; Elton Mayo conducts illumination experiments at Western Electric
1927	Mayo and others begin early-assembly test room study at the Hawthorne plant
1929	Great Depression; international scientific management conference held in France
1930	Hathaway, *Machining and Standard Times;* Allan H. Mogensen discusses 11 principles for work simplification in *Work Simplification*
1934	General Electric performs micromotion studies
1937	Ralph M. Barnes, *Motion and Time Study*
1941	R.L. Morrow, "Ratio Delay Study," in *Mechanical Engineering;* Fritz J. Roethlisberger, *Management and Morale*

1943   ASME work standardization committee publishes glossary of IE terms

1945   Kurt Lewin becomes director of MIT Group Dynamics Research Center; Marvin E. Mundel devises "memo-motion" study, a form of work measurement using time-lapse photography; Joseph H. Quick devises work factors (WF) method

1945   Shigeo Shingo presents concept of production as a network of processes and operations and identifies lot delays as source of delay between processes at a technical meeting of the Japan Management Association

1947   American mathematician, Norbert Wiener, *Cybernetics*

1948   H.B. Maynard and others introduce time measurement (MTM) method; Larry T. Miles develops value analysis (VA) at General Electric

1948   Shigeo Shingo announces process-based machine layout

1950   Mundel, *Motion and Time-Study Improving Productivity*

1951   Inductive statistical quality control introduced to Japan from United States

1952   Role and sampling study of IE conducted at ASME

1955   Shigeo Shingo presents production engineering lectures to Toyota Motor group; by 1986, some 6,000 students have attended

1956   New definition of industrial engineering offered at American Institute of Industrial Engineering convention

1957   Chris Argyris, *Personality and Organization;* Herbert A. Simon *Organizations;* R.L. Morrow, *Motion and Time Study*

1957	Shigeo Shingo introduces scientific thinking mechanism (STM) for improvements
1960	Douglas M. McGregor, *The Human Side of Enterprise*
1961	Rensis Lickert, *New Patterns of Management*
1961	Shigeo Shingo devises ZQC (source inspection and poka-yoke systems)
1963	Maynard, *IE Handbook;* Gerald Nadler, *Work Design*
1964	Abraham Maslow, *Motivation and Personality*
1966	Frederick Hertzberg, *Work and the Nature of Man*
1968	Roethlisberger, *Man in Organization;* U.S. Department of Defense, "Principles and Applications of Value Engineering"
1969	Shigeo Shingo develops single-minute exchange of dies (SMED)
1969	Shigeo Shingo introduces pre-automation
1971	Taiichi Ohno completes the Toyota Production System
1973	First annual systems engineering conference of AIIE is held
1975	Shigeo Shingo extols NSP-SS (non-stock production) system
1980	Matsushita Electric uses Mikuni method for washing machine production
1980	Shigeo Shingo, *Study of the Toyota Production System from an Industrial Engineering Viewpoint*
1981	First English edition of Shingo's *Study of the Toyota Production System* published in Japan
1984	Shigeo Shingo, *A Revolution in Manufacturing: The SMED System*

1985   Shigeo Shingo, *Zero Quality Control: Source Inspection and the Poka-yoke System*

1990   Shigeo Shingo, *The Shingo Production Management System*

Bibliography

Mr. Shingo's books have sold more than 40,000 copies worldwide. For convenience, all titles are given in English, although most have not yet been translated into English.

The improvement examples presented were drawn from Mr. Shingo's broad experience as a consultant. Many appear in his earlier works (in Japanese):

Technology for Plant Improvement. Japan Management Association, 1955.

Views and Thoughts on Plant Improvement and *Plant Improvement Embodiments and Examples,* a two-volume set published by Nikkan Kōgyō Shimbun, Ltd., 1957.

A Systematic Philosophy of Plant Improvement. Nikkan Kōgyō Shimbun, Ltd., 1980.

Mr. Shingo's other works include:

"Ten Strategies for Smashing Counterarguments," *Sakken to Kyoryoku* (Practice and Cooperation), 1938.

A General Introduction to Industrial Engineering. Japan Management Association, 1949.

Improving Production Control. Nihon Keizai Shimbun, 1950.

Production Control Handbook (Process Control). Kawade Shobō, 1953.

Don't Discard New Ideas. Hakuto Shobō, 1959.

Key Issues in Process Control Improvement. Nikkan Kōgyō Shimbun, Ltd., 1962.

Issues in Plant Improvement. Nikkan Kōgyō Shimbun, Ltd., 1964.

Techniques of Machine Layout Improvement. Nikkan Kōgyō Shimbun, Ltd., 1965.

Fundamental Approaches in Plant Improvement. Nikkan Kōgyō Shimbun, Ltd., 1976.

The Toyota Production System — An Industrial Engineering Study. Nikkan Kōgyō Shimbun, Ltd., 1980 (Also in English, French and Spanish.)

A Revolution in Manufacturing: The SMED System. Japan Management Association, 1983 (English edition Productivity Press, 1985).

Zero Quality Control: Source Inspection and the Poka-yoke System. Japan Management Association, 1985 (English edition Productivity Press, 1986).

The Sayings of Shigeo Shingo: Key Strategies for Plant Improvement. Nikkan Kōgyō Shimbun, Ltd., 1986 (English edition Productivity Press, 1987).

Non-Stock Production: The Shingo System for Continuous Improvement. Japan Management Association, 1987 (English edition Productivity Press, 1988).

A Study of the Toyota Production System from an Industrial Engineering Viewpoint. Japan Management Association, 1981 (newly translated and revised English edition Productivity Press, 1989).

Modern Approaches to Manufacturing Improvement: The Shingo System. Alan Robinson, Ed. (Productivity Press, 1990).

About the Author

CAREER: 50 YEARS IN FACTORY IMPROVEMENT

First Period: Private Enterprise

1909 Born in Saga City, Saga Prefecture, Japan, on January 8.

1924 While studying at Saga Technical High School, reads and is deeply impressed by Toshiro Ikeda's *The Secret of Eliminating Unprofitable Efforts*, said to be a translation of Taylor's thesis.

1930 Graduates from Yamanashi Technical College with a degree in mechanical engineering; goes to work for the Taipei Railway Factory.

1931 While a technician in the casting shop at the Taipei Railway Factory, observes worker operations and feels the need for improvement. Reads accounts of the streamlining of operations at Japan National Railways plants and awakens to the need for rational plant management.

Reads Taylor's *The Principles of Scientific Management* and, greatly impressed, decides to make the study and practice of scientific management his life's work.

Reads and studies many books, including the works of Yoichi Ueno and texts published by the Japan Industrial Association.

1937   For two months beginning September 1, attends the First Long-Term Industrial Engineering Training Course, sponsored by the Japan Industrial Association, the precursor of the Japan Management Association. Is thoroughly instructed in the "motion mind" concept by Ken'ichi Horikome.

1943   Transfers to the Amano Manufacturing Plant (Yokohama) on orders from the Ministry of Munitions. As Manufacturing Section Chief, applies flow operations to the processing of depth mechanisms for air-launched torpedoes and raises productivity by 100 percent.

Second Period: The Japan Management Association

1945   On orders from the Ministry of Munitions, transfers to Ishii Precision Mfg. (Niigata), a maker of similar air-launched torpedo depth mechanisms, for the purpose of improving factory operations.

With the end of the war in August, accepts a post at Yasui Kogyo (Kita Kyushu) starting in April 1946 and moves to Takanabe-cho in Miyazaki Prefecture. Stops by Tokyo at this time and visits Isamu Fukuda at the Japan Management Association, where he is introduced to Chairman of the Board Morikawa. Is asked to participate temporarily in a plant survey to improve operations at Hitachi, Ltd.'s, vehicle manufacturing facility at Kasado. Afterward enters the service of the Japan Management Association.

1946   When asked by a survey team member during process analysis at the Hitachi plant how to treat times when goods are delayed while waiting for cranes, realizes that "processes" and "operations," which had previously been thought to be separate and parallel entities, form a "network of processes and operations" — a systematic, synthetic whole. Reports this finding at a Japan Management Association technical conference.

Invents a method of classifying like operations by counting non-interventions while studying the layout of a Hitachi, Ltd., woodworking plant.

1948 Elucidates the "true nature of skill" in *A Study of 'Peko' Can Operations* at Toyo Steel's Shitamatsu plant.

Between 1948 and 1954, takes charge of Production Technology Courses. Also runs production technology classes at companies.

At a production technology course held at Hitachi, Ltd.'s, Fujita plant, begins to question the nature of plant layout. Studies and reflects on the problem.

1950 Perfects and implements a method for determining equipment layout based on a coefficient of ease of transport at Furukawa Electric's Copper Refinery in Nikko.

Analyzes work at a press at Tōyō Kōgyō and realizes that a setup operation is composed of "internal setup" (IED) and "external setup" (OED). This concept will become the first stage of SMED.

1954 Morita Masanobu from Toyota Motor Co., Ltd., participates in a production technology course at Toyoda Automatic Loom and achieves striking results when he returns to his company. This occasions a series of productivity technology courses inaugurated in 1955. By 1982, eighty-seven sessions of the course had been held, with approximately 2,000 participants.

1955 Observes multiple machine operations at the first production technology training course at Toyota Motor Corp. and is impressed by the separation of workers and machines.

1956 From 1956 to 1958 takes charge of a three-year study of Mitsubishi Shipbuilding's Nagasaki shipyards. Invents a new system for cutting supertanker assembly from four months to three and then to two. This system spreads to Japanese shipbuilding circles and contributes to the development of the shipbuilding industry.

1957 To raise the machining efficiency of an engine bed planer at Mitsubishi Shipbuilding's Hiroshima shipyards, constructs a spare table, conducts advance setup operations on it, and changes workpiece and table together. This doubles the work rate and foreshadows a crucially decisive conceptual element of SMED, that of shifting IED to EOD.

Third Period: The Institute for Management Improvement (Domestic)

1959 Leaves the Japan Management Association to found the Institute of Management Improvement.

1960 Originates the "successive inspection system" for reducing defects and implements the system at Matsushita Electric's Moriguchi plant.

1964 From Matsushita Electric's insistence that no level of defects is tolerable, realizes that, although selective inspection may be a rational procedure, it is not a rational means of assuring quality.

1965 Stimulated by Toyota Motor's "foolproof" production measures, eagerly seeks to eliminate defects entirely by systematically combining the concepts of successive inspection, independent inspection, and source inspection with "mistake-proof" techniques.

1966 Works as a business consultant to various Taiwanese firms, including Formosa Plastic Co., Matsushita Electric (Taiwan), and China Grinding Wheel Co. Consulted annually until 1981.

1969 Improves setup change for a 1,000-ton press at Toyota Motor's main plant from four hours to one and a half. Is soon afterward asked by management to cut setup time to three minutes and in a flash of insight thinks to shift IED to OED. With this, a systematic technique for achieving SMED is born.

Notices the difference between mechanization and automation when asked by Saga Ironworks' plant manager Yaya why automatic machines needed to be manned. This observation evolves into the concept of "pre-automation" which, Shingo later realizes, is identical to Toyota Motor's "autonomation."

1970 Is awarded the Yellow Ribbon Medal for contributions to streamlining operations in the shipbuilding industry, etc.

Fourth Period: The Institute for Management Improvement (International Expansion)

1971 Participates in observation tour of the European machine industry.

1973 Participates in observation tours of the machine industries in Europe and the United States.

1974 Lectures on SMED at die-cast industry associations in West Germany and Switzerland.

On this visit, observes vacuum die-casting methods at Daimler Benz in West Germany and Buehler in Switzerland and grows eager to implement vacuum molding in die-casting and plastic molding.

1975 Grows more enthusiastic about the "zero defects" concept on the basis of the achievement of zero defects in one month at the Shizuoka plant of Matsushita Electric's Washing Machine Operations Division.

Works for improvement based on fundamental approaches including high-speed plating, instantaneous drying, and the elimination of layout marking.

1976   Consults and lectures widely to promote SMED in Europe and the United States.

1977   Treats Toyota Motor's *kanban* system as essentially a scheme of "non-stock" production and develops systematic techniques for the system.

1978   Visits America's Federal-Mogul Corporation to provide on-site advice on SMED.

The sale by the Japan Management Association of an audio-visual set of slides on SMED and pre-automation meets with considerable success.

1979   Further success is attained by the Japan Management Association's sale of "zero defects" slides.

Visits Federal-Mogul to give follow-up guidance on SMED.

The collected results of Shingo's experiences and ideas concerning improvement are published.

1981   Makes two trips, in the spring and fall, to provide plant guidance to the French automobile manufacturers Peugeot and Citroen.

Travels to Australia to observe Toyota (Australia) and Borg-Warner.

1982   Makes follow-up consulting visits to Peugeot and Citroen in France and is impressed by the considerable results achieved through the application of SMED and non-stock production.

Consults and lectures at the Siemens company in Germany.

Lectures on "The Toyota Production System — An Industrial Engineering Study" in Munich.

Gives lectures at Chalmers University in Sweden.

Lectures at the University of Chicago.

1988 Lectures at Utah State University on his manufacturing methods for improving quality and productivity, and is awarded an honorary doctoral degree at that institution's commencement ceremonies.

Designates Utah State University as the center for annually awarding the "Shingo Prizes for Manufacturing Excellence" to North American businesses, students, and faculty.

Receives honorary doctoral degree from the Université de Toulouse in France.

1990 Active until the end, Shigeo Shingo dies peacefully on November 14 at the age of 81.

Index

Aiba, Toichi, 72
A Revolution in Manufacturing:
  The SMED System, 152
Argyris, Chris, 195
Asking "why," 30
Authorized production system
  (ASP), 38
Automobile door assembly, 103-4
Autonomation, 157

Babbage, Charles, 192
Barnes, Ralph M., 194
Barth, Carl G., 193
Batch operations, 16
Bed polishing, 101
Bell, Alexander Graham, 192
Bills, Daniel B., 19, 117
Block production, 130-33
Bodek, Norman, xxi, 189
Brainstorming, 50
Burrs, 71

Central Automobile KK, 86
Changeovers, 128-29
  See also Setup
Classification, 31-35

Clustered systems, 121-23
Communism, 183-84
Computers, 94-96
Control, management, 61-63
Cushion stock systems, 132-33

Daimler-Benz, 72, 80
Delay
  eliminating, 110-17
  types of, 99
Delivery cycle, 112
Demand, exploiting, 91-92
Die center marking, 100-101
Diemers, Hugo, 193

Edison, Thomas, 192
Emerson, Harrington, 193
Engineers, types of, 46-47

Fayol, Henri, 192
Fiat, 104
Five elements of production,
  36-38, 41
5W1H, 36-38, 41
Flow system, 120-21
Follet, Mary P., 194

211

Books from Productivity, Inc.

Productivity, Inc. publishes books that empower individuals and companies to achieve excellence in quality, productivity, and the creative involvement of all employees. Through steadfast efforts to support the vision and strategy of continuous improvement, Productivity, Inc. delivers today's leading-edge tools and techniques gathered directly from industrial leaders around the world. Call toll-free 1-800-394-6868 for our free catalog.

5 Pillars of the Visual Workplace
The Sourcebook for 5S Implementation
Hiroyuki Hirano

In this important sourcebook, JIT expert Hiroyuki Hirano provides the most vital information available on the visual workplace. He describes the 5S's: in Japanese they are seiri, seiton, seiso, seiketsu, and shitsuke (which translate as sort, set in order, shine, standardize, and sustain). Hirano discusses how the 5S theory fosters efficiency, maintenance, and continuous improvement in all areas of the company, from the plant floor to the sales office. This book includes case material, graphic illustrations, and photographs.
ISBN 1-56327-047-1 / 377 pages, illustrated / $85.00 / Order FIVE-B219

20 Keys to Workplace Improvement
Iwao Kobayashi

The 20 Keys system does more than just bring together twenty of the world's top manufacturing improvement approaches—it integrates these individual methods into a closely interrelated system for revolutionizing every aspect of your manufacturing organization. This revised edition of Kobayashi's best-seller amplifies the synergistic power of raising the levels of all these critical areas simultaneously. The new edition presents upgraded criteria for the five-level scoring system in most of the 20 Keys, supporting your progress toward becoming not only best in your industry but best in the world. New material and an updated layout throughout assist managers in implementing this comprehensive approach. In addition, valuable case studies describe how Morioka Seiko (Japan) advanced in Key 18 (use of microprocessors) and how Windfall Products (Pennsylvania) adapted the 20 Keys to its situation with good results.
ISBN 1-56327-109-5 / 304 pages / $50.00 / Order 20KREV-B219

40 Top Tools for Manufacturers
A Guide for Implementing Powerful Improvement Activities
Walter Michalski

We know how important it is for you to have the right tool when you need it. And if you're a team leader or facilitator in a manufacturing environment, you've probably been searching a long time for a collection of implementation tools tailored specifically to your needs. Well, look no further. Based on the same principles and user-friendly design of *Tool Navigator: The Master Guide for Teams*, here is a group of 40 dynamic tools to help you and your teams implement powerful manufacturing process improvement. Use this essential resource to select, sequence, and apply major TQM tools, methods, and processes.
ISBN 1-56327-197-4 / 160 pages / $25.00 / Order NAV2-B219

Becoming Lean
Inside Stories of U.S. Manufacturers
Jeffrey Liker

Most other books on lean management focus on technical methods and offer a picture of what a lean system should look like. Some provide snapshots of before and after. This is the first book to provide technical descriptions of successful solutions and performance improvements. The first book to include powerful first-hand accounts of the complete process of change, its impact on the entire organization, and the rewards and benefits of becoming lean. At the heart of this book you will find the stories of American manufacturers who have successfully implemented lean methods. Authors offer personalized accounts of their organization's lean transformation, including struggles and successes, frustrations and surprises. Now you have a unique opportunity to go inside their implementation process to see what worked, what didn't, and why. Many of these executives and managers who led the charge to becoming lean in their organizations tell their stories here for the first time!
ISBN 1-56327-173-7 / 350 pages / $35.00 / Order LEAN-B219

Building a Shared Vision
A Leader's Guide to Aligning the Organization
C. Patrick Lewis

This exciting new book presents a step-by-step method for developing your organizational vision. It teaches how to build and maintain a shared vision directed from the top down, but encompassing the views of all the members and stakeholders, and understanding the competitive environment of the organization. Like Corporate Diagnosis, this books describes in detail one of the necessary first steps from Implementing a Lean Management System: visioning.
ISBN 1-56327-163-X / 150 pages / $45.00 / Order VISION- B219

PRODUCTIVITY, INC., DEPT. BK, P.O. BOX 13390, PORTLAND, OR 97213-0390
Telephone: 1-800-394-6868   Fax: 1-800-394-6286

Building Organizational Fitness
Management Methodology for Transformation and Strategic Advantage
Ryuji Fukuda

The most urgent task for companies today is to take a hard look at the future. To remain competitive, management must nurture a strong capability for self-development and a strong corporate culture, both of which form part of the foundation for improvement. But simply understanding management techniques doesn't mean you know how to use them. You need the tools and technologies for implementation. In Building Organizational Fitness, Fukuda extends the power of his managerial engineering methodology into the context of the top management strategic planning role.
ISBN 1-56327-144-3 / 250 pages / $65.00 / Order BFIT-B219

Eliminating Minor Stoppages on Automated Lines
Kikuo Suehiro

Stoppages of automated equipment lines severely affect productivity, cost, and lead time. Such losses make decreasing the number of stoppages a crucial element of TPM. Kikuo Suehiro has helped companies such as Hitachi achieve unprecedented reduction in the number of minor stoppages. In this explicitly detailed book, he presents a scientific approach to determining the causes of stoppages and the actions that can be taken to diminish their occurrence.
ISBN 0-915299-70-4 / 243 pages / $50.00 / Order ELIM-B219

Handbook for Productivity Measurement and Improvement
William F. Christopher and Carl G. Thor, eds.

An unparalleled resource! In over 100 chapters, nearly 80 front-runners in the quality movement reveal the evolving theory and specific practices of world-class organizations. Spanning a wide variety of industries and business sectors, they discuss quality and productivity in manufacturing, service industries, profit centers, administration, nonprofit and government institutions, health care and education. Contributors include Robert C. Camp, Peter F. Drucker, Jay W. Forrester, Joseph M. Juran, Robert S. Kaplan, John W. Kendrick, Yasuhiro Monden, and Lester C. Thurow. Comprehensive in scope and organized for easy reference, this compendium belongs in every company and academic institution concerned with business and industrial viability.
ISBN 1-56327-007-2 / 1344 pages / $90.00 / Order HPM-B219

PRODUCTIVITY, INC., DEPT. BK, P.O. BOX 13390, PORTLAND, OR 97213-0390
Telephone: 1-800-394-6868   Fax: 1-800-394-6286

The Hunters and the Hunted
A Non-Linear Solution for Reengineering the Workplace
James B. Swartz

Our competitive environment changes rapidly. If you want to survive, you have to stay on top of those changes. Otherwise, you become prey to your competitors. Hunters continuously change and learn; anyone who doesn't becomes the hunted and sooner or later will be devoured. This unusual non-fiction novel provides a veritable crash course in continuous transformation. It offers lessons from real-life companies and introduces many industrial gurus as characters. The Hunters and the Hunted doesn't simply tell you how to change; it puts you inside the change process itself.
ISBN 1-56327-043-9 / 564 pages / $45.00 / Order HUNT-B219

JIT Factory Revolution
A Pictorial Guide to Factory Design of the Future
Hiroyuki Hirano

The first encyclopedic picture-book of Just-In-Time, using photos and diagrams to show exactly how JIT looks and functions in production and assembly plants. Unprecedented behind-the-scenes look at multiprocess handling, cell technology, quick changeovers, kanban, andon, and other visual control systems. See why a picture is worth a thousand words.
ISBN 0-915299-44-5 / 218 pages / $50.00 / Order JITFAC-B219

Quick Response Manufacturing
A Companywide Approach to Reducing Lead Times
Rajan Suri

Quick Response Manufacturing (QRM) is an expansion of time-based competition (TBC) strategies which use speed for a competitive advantage. Essentially, QRM stems from a single principle: to reduce lead times. But unlike other time-based competition strategies, QRM is an approach for the entire organization, from the front desk to the shop floor, from purchasing to sales. In order to truly succeed with speed-based competition, you must adopt the approach *throughout* the organization.
ISBN 1-56327-201-6/ 560 pages / $50.00 / Order QRM-B219

A Revolution in Manufacturing
The SMED System
Shigeo Shingo

The heart of JIT is quick changeover methods. Dr. Shingo, inventor of the Single-Minute Exchange of Die (SMED) system for Toyota, shows you how to reduce your changeovers by an average of 98 percent! By applying Shingo's techniques, you'll see rapid improvements (lead time reduced from weeks to days, lower inventory and warehousing costs) that will improve quality, productivity, and profits.
ISBN 0-915299-03-8 / 383 pages / $80.00 / Order SMED-B219

PRODUCTIVITY, INC., DEPT. BK, P.O. BOX 13390, PORTLAND, OR 97213-0390
Telephone: 1-800-394-6868   Fax: 1-800-394-6286

The Sayings of Shigeo Shingo
Key Strategies for Plant Improvement
Shigeo Shingo

Quality Digest calls Shigeo Shingo "an unquestioned genius—the Thomas Edison of Japan." Shingo "offers new ways to discover the root causes of manufacturing problems. These discoveries can set in motion the chain of cause and effect, leading to greatly increased productivity." Hundreds of examples illustrate ways to identify, analyze and solve workplace problems.
ISBN 0-915299-15-1 / 207 pages / $45.00 / Order SAY-B219

A Study of the Toyota Production System from an Industrial Engineering Viewpoint
Shigeo Shingo

Here is Dr. Shingo's classic industrial engineering rationale for the priority of process-based over operational improvements for manufacturing. He explains the basic mechanisms of the Toyota production system in a practical and simple way so that you can apply them in your own plant. This book clarifies the fundamental principles of JIT including levelling, standard work procedures, multi-machine handling, and more.
ISBN 0-915299-17-8 / 291 pages / $45.00 / Order STREV-B219

Toyota Production System
Beyond Large-Scale Production
Taiichi Ohno

Here's the first information ever published in Japan on the Toyota production system (known as Just-In-Time manufacturing). Here Ohno, who created JIT for Toyota, reveals the origins, daring innovations, and ceaseless evolution of the Toyota system into a full management system. You'll learn how to manage JIT from the man who invented it, and to create a winning JIT environment in your own manufacturing operation.
ISBN 0-915299-14-3 / 163 pages / $45.00 / Order OTPS-B219

The Visual Factory
Building Participation Through Shared Information
Michel Greif

If you're aware of the tremendous improvements achieved in productivity and quality as a result of employee involvement, then you'll appreciate the great value of creating a visual factory. This book shows how visual management can make the factory a place where workers and supervisors freely communicate and take improvement action. It details how to develop meeting and communication areas, communicate work standards and instructions, use visual production controls such as kanban, and make goals and progress visible. Includes more than 200 diagrams and photos.
ISBN 0-915299-67-4 / 305 pages / $55.00 / Order VFAC-B219

PRODUCTIVITY, INC., DEPT. BK, P.O. BOX 13390, PORTLAND, OR 97213-0390
Telephone: 1-800-394-6868   Fax: 1-800-394-6286

Zero Quality Control
Source Inspection and the Poka-Yoke System
Shigeo Shingo

Dr. Shingo reveals his unique defect prevention system, which combines source inspection and poka-yoke (mistake-proofing) devices that provide instant feedback on errors before they can become defects. The result: 100 percent inspection that eliminates the need for SQC and produces defect-free products without fail. Includes 112 examples, most costing under $100. Two-part video program also available; call for details.
ISBN 0-915299-07-0 / 328 pages / $75.00 / Order ZQC-B219

TO ORDER: Write, phone, or fax Productivity, Inc., Dept. BK, P.O. Box 13390, Portland, OR 97213-0390, phone 1-800-394-6868, fax 1-800-394-6286. Send check or charge to your credit card (American Express, Visa, MasterCard accepted).

U.S. ORDERS: Add $5 shipping for first book, $2 each additional for UPS surface delivery. Add $5 for each AV program containing 1 or 2 tapes; add $15 for each AV program containing 3 or more tapes. We offer attractive quantity discounts for bulk purchases of individual or mixed titles; call for more information.

ORDER BY E-MAIL: Order 24 hours a day from anywhere in the world. Use either address:
To order: **info@productivityinc.com**
To view the online catalog and/or order: **http://www.productivityinc.com/**
QUANTITY DISCOUNTS: For information on quantity discounts, please contact our sales department.

INTERNATIONAL ORDERS: Write, phone, or fax for quote and indicate shipping method desired. For international callers, the telephone number is 503-235-0600 and the fax number is 503-235-0909. Prepayment in U.S. dollars must accompany your order (checks must be drawn on U.S. banks). When quote is returned with payment, your order will be shipped promptly by the method requested.

NOTE: *Prices are in U.S. dollars and are subject to change without notice.*

PRODUCTIVITY, INC., DEPT. BK, P.O. BOX 13390, PORTLAND, OR 97213-0390
Telephone: 1-800-394-6868   Fax: 1-800-394-6286

ABOUT THE SHOPFLOOR SERIES

Put powerful and proven improvement tools in the hands of your entire workforce! Progressive shopfloor improvement techniques are imperative for manufacturers who want to stay competitive and to achieve world class excellence. And it's the comprehensive education of all shopfloor workers that ensures full participation and success when implementing new programs. The Shopfloor Series books make practical information accessible to everyone by presenting major concepts and tools in simple, clear language and at a reading level that has been adjusted for operators by skilled instructional designers. One main idea is presented every two to four pages so that the book can be picked up and put down easily. Each chapter begins with an overview and ends with a summary section. Helpful illustrations are used throughout.

Books currently in the Shopfloor Series include:

5S for Operators
5 Pillars of the Visual Workplace
The Productivity Press Development Team
ISBN 1-56327-123-0
incl. application questions / 133 pages
Order # 5SOP-B219 / $25.00

Quick Changeover for Operators
The SMED System
The Productivity Press Development Team
ISBN 1-56327-125-7
incl. application questions / 93 pages
Order # QCOOP-B219 / $25.00

Mistake-Proofing for Operators
The Productivity Press Development Team
ISBN 1-56327-127-3 / 93 pages
Order # ZQCOP-B219 / $25.00

Just-In-Time for Operators
The Productivity Press Development Team
ISBN 1-56327-133-8 / 96 pages
Order # JITOP-B219 / $25.00

TPM for Supervisors
The Productivity Press Development Team
ISBN 1-56327-161-3 / 96 pages
Order # TPMSUP-B219 / $25.00

TPM Team Guide
Kunio Shirose
ISBN 1-56327-079-X / 175 pages
Order # TGUIDE-B219 / $25.00

Autonomous Maintenance
Japan Institute of Plant Maintenance
ISBN 1-56327-082-X / 138 pages
Order # AUTMOP-B219 / $25.00

Focused Equipment Improvement
Japan Institute of Plant Maintenance
ISBN 1-56327-081-1 / 138 pages
Order # FEIOP-B219 / $25.00

TPM for Every Operator
Japan Institute of Plant Maintenance
ISBN 1-56327-080-3 / 136 pages
Order # TPMEO-B219 / $25.00

OEE for Operators
Overall Equipment Effectiveness
The Productivity Press Development Team
ISBN 1-56327-082-X / 138 pages
Order # AUTMOP-B219 / $25.00

Cellular Manufacturing
The Productivity Press Development Team
ISBN 1-56327-213-X / 96 pages
Order # CELLP-B219 / $25.00

PRODUCTIVITY, INC., DEPT. BK, P.O. BOX 13390, PORTLAND, OR 97213-0390
Telephone: 1-800-394-6868   Fax: 1-800-394-6286

Productivity, Inc. Consulting, Training, Workshops, and Conferences

EDUCATION...IMPLEMENTATION...RESULTS

Productivity, Inc. is the leading American consulting, training, and publishing company focusing on delivering improvement technology to the global manufacturing industry.

Productivity prides itself on delivering today's leading performance improvement tools and methodologies to enhance rapid, ongoing, measurable results. Whether you need assistance with long-term planning or focused, results-driven training, Productivity's world-class consultants can enhance your pursuit of competitive advantage. In concert with your management team, Productivity will focus on implementing the principles of Value-Adding Management, Total Quality Management, Just-in-Time, and Total Productive Maintenance. Each approach is supported by Productivity's wide array of team-based tools: Standardization, One-Piece Flow, Hoshin Planning, Quick Changeover, Mistake-Proofing, Kanban, Problem Solving with CEDAC, Visual Workplace, Visual Office, Autonomous Maintenance, Overall Equipment Effectiveness, Design of Experiments, Quality Function Deployment, Ergonomics, and more! And, based on continuing research, Productivity expands its offering every year.

Productivity's conferences provide an excellent opportunity to interact with the best of the best. Each year our national conferences bring together the leading practitioners of world-class, high-performance strategies. Our workshops, forums, plant tours, and master series are scheduled throughout the U.S. to provide the opportunity for continuous improvement in key areas of lean management and production.

Productivity, Inc. is known for significant improvement on the shop floor and the bottom line. Through years of repeat business, an expanding and loyal client base continues to recommend Productivity to their colleagues. Contact us at 1-800-394-6868 to learn how we can tailor our services to fit your needs.